Griffin

Greater Attention

Greater Attention

Liturgical Elements for Reformed Worship

━ YEAR D ━

TIMOTHY MATTHEW SLEMMONS

CASCADE *Books* · Eugene, Oregon

GREATER ATTENTION
Liturgical Elements for Reformed Worship, Year D

Cascade Books
An Imprint of Wipf and Stock Publishers
199 W. 8th Ave., Suite 3
Eugene, OR 97401

www.wipfandstock.com

ISBN 13: 978–1–62032–003–7

Cataloguing-in-Publication Data

Slemmons, Timothy Matthew.

Greater attention : liturgical elements for reformed worship, year d / Timothy Matthew Slemmons.

xxvi + 232 pp. ; 23 cm. Includes index.

ISBN 13: 978–1–62032–003–7

1. Reformed Church—Liturgy—Handbooks, manuals, etc. 2. Common lectionary (1992). Year D—Handbooks, manuals, etc. 3. Reformed Church—Liturgy. 4. Lectionaries—Handbooks, manuals, etc. I. Title.

BX9427 .S44 2013

Manufactured in the U.S.A.

*Dedicated to the glory of the triune God
for the gift of my beloved wife*

—Victoria Beth Slemmons—

*and in honor of her sweet Christian spirit,
her gifts of prayer, harp, and song,
and her countless acts of kindness and love.*

"*Therefore we must pay greater attention to what we have heard, so that we do not drift away from it. For if the message declared through angels was valid, and every transgression or disobedience received a just penalty, how can we escape if we neglect so great a salvation?*"

Hebrews 2:1–3a (First Sunday of Advent)

Contents

Part II: The Paschal Cycle: *Lent—Easter—Pentecost*

Part III: Ordinary Time (Propers 4–29):
Trinity—All Saints'—Christ the King

Series Foreword

THIS SERIES OF *LITURGICAL ELEMENTS FOR REFORMED WORSHIP* HAS developed over the course of more than fifteen years of ministry in Presbyterian contexts, primarily pastoral but also academic. Although this development has coincided with my own vocational (theological, homiletical, liturgical, and pastoral) formation and will therefore reflect a number of vocal variations (so to speak) that correspond to different stages of this formation, the primary concern that gave rise to this project in the first place has not diminished in the least, but has taken on an even deeper and more persistent sense of gravity and conviction. What began as a practical search for a greater variety of prayers of confession and assurances than I found in the *Book of Common Worship* (1993)—and more specifically, for prayers that reflected more directly how the Church should confess in response to specific texts found in the *Revised Common Lectionary* (1992) from week to week—has become an overriding concern that informs both my work in advocating an expansion of the lectionary, as well as my labors in the area of Reformed homiletics and worship, namely, that ongoing and continual repentance from sin in all its forms is essential, not accidental, to the Christian life, to the Reformed tradition of worship, and to the vitality and viability of the Church.

Reared as so many other pastors and seminary students have been on the textbooks of the late liturgical scholar James F. White, an ecumenically minded Methodist who served on the faculty at Notre Dame, I too quickly and uncritically adopted White's dim characterization of Reformed worship that he repeatedly describes (at least in the hands of the Swiss Reformers and their Calvinist and Puritan descendants) as "heavily penitential." This negative caricature is reinforced so often by White[1] and in the literature developed in his wake that his more posi-

1. James F. White, *Introduction to Christian Worship*, 3rd ed. (Nashville: Abingdon, 2000) 124, 160, 161, 189, 254, 256, et al., and *A Brief History of Christian Worship*

tive assessment of the joy with which the same tradition sang the Psalms seems jarringly inconsistent, that is, as though the connection between repentance and the joyful freedom to be discovered therein is entirely incongruous. Equally symptomatic of White's failure to appreciate the Reformed tradition is his suggestion that Calvin simply followed the Fourth Lateran Council in requiring confession before communion, as though the premier theologian of the sixteenth century applied the scriptural regulative principle to every question but this one.

White was not alone in his superficial (i.e., dour) understanding of the Reformed tradition, of course, but his conviction that "the study of Christian worship is the best way to learn ecumenism" has been influential and probably explains why many Reformed liturgical scholars today seem more eager to shun whatever may be described as "heavily penitential" than to lay claim to the true character of the Reformed tradition as *essentially* penitential, and not merely in a manner that belongs to the medieval period, from which, the ecumenist White suggests, the Reformers were not sufficiently critical to separate themselves. On the contrary, the point that should appear obvious to those who apply the principle of canonical comprehensiveness[2] in their study of Scripture and the regulative principle to their study of the Reformation is that the Reformers, in their own exegetical labors, discerned the summons to repentance resounding throughout the canon and (despite important differences in grammatical moods) on both sides of the crucifixion, resurrection, and ascension of Jesus, and they felt sufficiently convinced and convicted by it that they sought to give it a central and essential, not an auxiliary role, in their liturgical reforms. As I have said elsewhere, this essential role of repentance is signaled at least symbolically, and perhaps definitively, in the fact that the first of Luther's ninety-five theses (1517), the initial downbeat of the Reformation itself, declares that the Christian life is one of ongoing repentance. Meanwhile, the liturgical renewal movement, driven in part by the desire to avoid medieval stereotypes, has succeeded in depriving the Reformed worship tradition of one of its greatest, most distinctive, and powerful gifts: the disciplines of self-examination and robust confession that are the hallmark of true repentance and deep "reform." The services of preparation and self-examination (that last appeared in the

---

(Nashville: Abingdon, 1993) 76, 105, et al.

2. See Timothy Matthew Slemmons, *Year D: A Quadrennial Supplement to the Revised Common Lectionary* (Eugene, OR: Cascade, 2012).

1946 edition of the *Book of Common Worship*) have given way before the drive toward more frequent communion, and one can only wonder at what point, if ever, the trend toward less preparation and more "celebration" will bring to mind the long forgotten and much abused dialectic of the holy and the common.

It is from this point of deep conviction that this series of liturgical resources is sent forth, not because every element will necessarily do justice to the sense in which perpetual repentance is the most frequently overlooked and distinctive "essential tenet" of the Reformed tradition (and because the most distinctive, therefore the most essential, so to speak), but for the simple fact that repentance, self-examination, confession, and the good news of forgiveness deserve far better than to be reduced to the formulaic. It may well be that those who worship in the Reformed tradition, at least those who are unembarrassed by the essentially penitential—and undeniably joyful—character of the tradition, are best positioned to lay claim to that truth and offer it to the broader Church. On the other hand, anyone who would persist in such embarrassment, I would suggest, is not paying sufficient attention—to Scripture, to the state of the Church, to the state of the world, or the state of their own souls.

This is not to say that these elements come from on high, by any stretch, except insofar as they are a response to, and sometimes a direct voicing of, Scripture. Rather, these prayers come from the pen of one who needs to pray them. They were in no instance designed to be prescriptive, but are the best response this pastor has been able to muster as one who finds himself staring down the business end of the sword of the Word (Eph 6:17; Heb 4:12; Rev 2:12; 19:15, 21). But what a startling thing it was the first time I heard a congregation praying in unison a Prayer of Confession I had written and printed in the bulletin! Having shifted my focus entirely from the task of getting the bulletin together on Thursday afternoon to entering into worship itself on Sunday morning, I was halfway through the prayer myself before I realized: "These words sound familiar." Then it dawned on me: "Oh, yes. I wrote them."

There was nothing especially gratifying about this experience, for I have never harbored any great aspiration to put words in other people's mouths. But from that moment the prospect of writing prayers that the people of God themselves would speak in worship became a particularly sobering and serious responsibility. For, in fact, there is an inescapable sense in which "finding words for worship"[3] does in effect put words in the mouths of those in attendance: individuals of innumerable dispositions, including some who may well resist assenting (saying "Amen") to them, and churches (local, denominational, and global) whose spiritual and moral conditions need to be truthfully and honestly confessed in the presence of "God and everybody." It is no exaggeration whatsoever, but theologically and anthropologically accurate, to say that the Prayer of Confession can, by its very nature as an expression and an act of repentance, "make one's flesh crawl," for repentance is a gift from God (Acts 5:31; 11:18), but "the mind that is set on the flesh is hostile to God; it does not submit to God's law—indeed it cannot . . ." (Rom 8:6–7). Prayers of Confession then must walk a fine line, balancing "brutal" honesty with tender mercy; they must break the horse, not make it bolt.

The responsibility for liturgy is incalculably heightened when one considers that such prompting of the people is no mere stage direction; yet, per Kierkegaard's *contra*-theatrical analogy, the minister or preacher *is* a prompter whose labor is done with the expectation that the people will in fact direct the prompted words *to* God. And as if *this* were not enough, the pastor and liturgist must remember that the liturgy at points entails speaking *for* God to the people—as in the Declaration of Forgiveness, which bears the liberating function of Gospel every bit as much as does the preaching of the Word. *God* calls the people to worship. *The risen Jesus Christ* heralds the good news of forgiveness. Worship is less a work of the people (who are but the minor partners in the conversation) and more a work of *the Holy Spirit*. Yet *the Holy Trinity* condescends to enlist human agents in doing all of this work (externally speaking), much of it through the pastor as liturgist. Sobering thoughts indeed.

But such a responsibility cannot be fulfilled by a formulaic approach. The routinization of worship is deadly, even if it results from the most faithful allegiance to orthodoxy. As one pastoral colleague put the problem when I entered into this project some fifteen years ago, "So how many ways can you say, 'You are forgiven!'?" That is certainly one way of posing the question. How should one answer? To begin with: more than three.[4] On the one hand, the words of Scripture themselves are the sole written authority and norm for all elements of worship, including the Declaration

3. See Ruth Duck, *Finding Words for Worship: A Guide for Leaders* (Louisville: Westminster John Knox, 1995).

4. *Book of Common Worship* (Louisville: Westminster John Knox, 1993) 56–57.

of Forgiveness. On the other hand, the same Spirit who speaks through the Scriptures resists distillation of the singular gospel to a single formula, but inspires ongoing interpretation, reiteration, amplification, and elaboration as required by a wide variety of human conditions; for sin, depravity, guilt, pride, and all manner of things that exalt themselves in opposition to the Word (2 Cor 10:4) may succeed against incantation, but they will not succeed against the Church at worship recapitulating the *missio Dei* in fresh, biblically faithful ways. The Word of the LORD will not return empty (Isa 55), and the gates of hell will not prevail against the Church (Matt 16) *at worship*. As J.-J. von Allmen observed (specifically with reference to 1 Cor 11–14), the term *ecclesia* first and foremost applies to the liturgical assembly; it is not primarily a sociological term.[5] This insight, clear as it is in Scripture, has yet to sink in to the mind of the mainline churches, which seem entirely bent on sociological reform. But if von Allmen was right, and I think he was, then I would contend that the diversity of the Church need not be forced to satisfy our sociological presuppositions, whether liberal or conservative, but allowed to arise in and emerge from worship itself as the Church encounters the risen Christ and the Holy Spirit speaking through the Scriptures.

Further, if we follow this understanding of an essentially liturgical ecclesiology, and an essentially repentant orientation to the Christian life, through to their logical conclusion and point of convergence, we must finally recognize the fact that, in the temporal sphere (and whether we like it or not), Christian worship cannot be fully grasped apart from the theatre of spiritual warfare by which it is surrounded and from which it is protected and held *in God* as a sanctuary—a holy "safe" zone, so to speak—an assembly around font, pulpit, and table, with the whole creation (Rom 8:19), even a host of impotent enemies (Ps 23:5), looking on.

"Safe," of course, is a relative term and begs definition in relation to its distinct referents. I would not be so naïve in this day and age to suggest that physical harm cannot come to God's people in worship, but I shall say with the psalmist, "I trust in God; I am not afraid; what can flesh do to me?" (Ps 56:4) Neither would I suggest that the holy presence of God is unambiguously "safe," so as to lose sight of the "fear of the LORD" that is due him (Ps 90:11). Nevertheless, when worship is framed in this way, the Church stands to gain a much clearer sense of what is at stake, and to

5. J.-J. von Allmen, *Worship: Its Theology and Practice* (New York: Oxford University Press, 1965) 43.

see people of every spiritual condition avail themselves of the healing and salvific presence of the Lord, even as worship itself serves (esthetically) as creation's libretto in the theatre of God's glory, the theatre in which "the battle is the LORD's" and the Church's vocation is to remember and give thanks for victories past and promised. As von Allmen held:

> in its liturgy the Church acts on behalf of the world, which is totally
> incapable of adoring and glorifying the true God, and . . . the Church
> [at worship] represents the world before God and protects it.[6]

In other words, the Church, as a royal priesthood in Christ, has an inter-cessory role to play whereby its worship, as it were, actually "protects" the world. That alone should be both good news to the whole Church and good news to the world! Hence, liturgy is really not "common worship" in any sense. On the contrary, liturgy is the divine and priestly service of the body of Christ, the service of worship performed by the Church—as it is empowered, guided, and inspired by the Holy Spirit—for God and in response to God's gracious self-revelation in the Servant Lord Jesus Christ. True liturgy unfolds under the headship, under the most excellent ministry (liturgy), and in the name of Jesus Christ, the Son of God, in whom all believers together are to serve in a united yet diversely gifted priesthood, to the eternal glory of God—and (temporarily) on behalf of a liturgically incompetent and often hostile world.

These convictions, as mentioned above, have come very slowly.[7] While I hope in future to be able to articulate these concerns and convic-tions more clearly and thoroughly (and defend them, if necessary), for now I must admit the evidence of this unlovely developmental plodding may be all too obvious in the liturgical elements provided here and in the three companion volumes that are planned. For this project has developed contemporaneously with my own continuing theological education and vocation, and in the weekly attempt to prepare faithful worship amidst the numerous competing demands of life and ministry; thus, all stages of this development will be represented here. This will account for the varying degrees of tone: from solemnity to exuberance, from the poetic to the prosaic, from an initial concern for avoiding overuse of masculine metaphors for God to a more intentional use of the biblical names of God,

6 Ibid., 16.

7. As I say frequently and with no irony intended, I loosely translate the Latin on my own PhD (*philosophiae doctor*) degree to read, "slow learner."

including Lᴏʀᴅ and Lord, etc., and a desire to avoid the far greater sin of effectively depersonalizing God by the avoidance of personal pronouns. (Where the use of Lᴏʀᴅ is concerned, my intention has been to retain this reference to the tetragrammaton, YHWH, as it is rendered in most translations of the Old Testament, and thereby direct the reader's attention to the holy name as it is used in the texts that inspired the element in question; likewise, the use of Lord is meant to reflect usage in the New Testament, which most often occurs in reference to Jesus.) In light of this peculiarly developmental quality, then, the reader may find it more helpful to approach these volumes as more of an indicative historical record, as useful artifacts, than as prescriptive in any heavy-handed or "heavily penitential" sense. They are perhaps a tidy presentation of the otherwise untidy relics of many services, a peek into one pastor's file drawers stuffed with bulletins and prayers prepared for congregations perhaps very different from the reader's own. Many, if not most, of these elements, if they are to be of service to the ongoing life of the Church at worship, will invite adaptation, in which case I simply ask that those who thus adapt them will acknowledge doing so, yet remember with kindness and favor the congregations, both the saints and their pastor, whence and among whom—by the grace of the Word and the Spirit—they first arose.

Timothy Matthew Slemmons
University of Dubuque Theological Seminary
The Feast of Epiphany, A.D. 2012

Preface

THE FOURTH (PRESENT) VOLUME IN THIS PLANNED SERIES OF *LITURGICAL Elements for Reformed Worship* differs from the others in two major respects. First, it ventures beyond the current confines of the *Revised Common Lectionary* in its effort to support the use of Year D as a quadrennial or *ad hoc* supplement to its three-year cycle.[8] The reason for this departure derives largely from the concerns that have given rise to the design of Year D itself. These concerns are, briefly: (1) the conviction that the state of decline of the mainline church in North America will not be reversed by any human strategy, whether social, ideological, rhetorical, or otherwise, but only by the agency of the Word and the Spirit of God; (2) the sense in which this conviction is no mere theoretical premise, but may and must be worked out in worship itself at the most pragmatic level when the Word of God is actually *used* as such and thereby gains fresh utterance in reading, preaching, prayer, and song; (3) the evident fact that the alarming decline in the health of the (ecclesial and organic) body of Christ, at least in the mainline, is a matter of an acquired imbalance in our corporate diet of Scripture; (4) the chorus of scriptural voices, in every canonical genre, that insist upon giving attention to and honoring the totality of God's revelation; and (5) the obvious implication, from all the above, that the "patient" requires an orderly application of missing nutrients for the sake of restoring health to the body.

The second way in which this fourth volume differs is that its focus is primarily on the Gathering, i.e., the opening elements of the entrance and penitential rites, while the elements themselves are often longer, and make more direct use of Scripture. There are several reasons why the Gathering receives peculiar emphasis. First and most obvious is simply the lack of any extant liturgical resources to support the introduction

8. Timothy Matthew Slemmons, *Year D: A Quadrennial Supplement to the Revised Common Lectionary* (Eugene, OR: Cascade, 2012).

and deployment of the texts that comprise Year D. The Gathering rites, of course, afford the first and primary opportunity to give the people of God access via these texts to worship that is formed and informed by their particular theological emphases and perspectives. The task of the entrance and penitential rites, as I understand them, is to lead the people into the holy presence (or into an *awareness* of the holy presence) of the Triune God, and it is there, in that encounter, that these texts may best be considered, understood, interpreted, and applied to the Christian life.

Another reason for this peculiar focus is that, while the same penitential considerations discussed in the Series Forward apply here, what one soon discovers in the texts that comprise Year D (i.e., texts that have been omitted from the *RCL*) is that the reasons for, or "calls" to, confession and ongoing repentance abound, while fresh statements of grace and good news are likewise abundant. If the former outweigh the latter, then let the record show that this distortion is traceable to the biases in the *RCL* itself, rather than to Year D, which is designed in direct response and with reference to the extant lectionary. If these elements appears overly lengthy, full, or even fulsome, this is due to: (1) the scale, scope, and bulk of the lectionary's redactions, and (2) both "the need and the promise" of the same material to function for the glory of God and for the reforming benefit to the individual and to the worshipping assembly. Put another way, we should not be surprised that when repressed voices finally get a chance to speak, they have a lot to say. Similarly, when it comes to repressed texts in the written (but, for generations, unvoiced) word of God, we likewise expect they will have a lot of work to do.

For these reasons, I will continue to advocate for the full integration of Year D to the preaching rotation in lectionary-based congregations, and voice my hope and prayer that, while the present volume is the first resource of its kind, it will by no means be the last. Its aim, in short, is to usher people into the presence of these texts . . . and of God via these texts. What the preacher should preach once there, how the congregation should respond, intercede, and engage in mission: these considerations are beyond the scope of this present resource and belong to the daily and weekly disciplines of exegesis, worship, planning, sermon preparation, and the pastoral life. A good place to start, however, would be with the concise commentary in *Year D: A Quadrennial Supplement* itself.

Where future Year D resources are concerned, I would welcome, invite, and encourage others to develop educational curricula, musical resources, theological, exegetical, and homiletical commentaries to support the use of these texts. Additional liturgical resources in pastoral voices other than my own would certainly be appropriate, and, it is expected, will ring with perhaps less of the urgency of the "first responder" than the elements contained herein, and with a higher sense of esthetic beauty and grace. Meanwhile, may this resource render the use of Year D all the more practical by pastors, preachers, liturgists, worship leaders, and worship committees, and may it remove the primary obstacle to the systematic introduction of these texts of which, as the Lord knows best, the churches are in dire need.

Where the subtitle and epigraph of this volume are concerned, the scriptural summons to "pay greater attention" (Heb 2:1–3) likely needs no further explanation beyond that which I have already mentioned in the *Quadrennial Supplement*. Nevertheless, it is worth reiterating that this call to attention constitutes the first word of Year D in the course of the epistle readings (First Sunday of Advent). The reason for its prominence is not simply that it is the first missing piece (omitted from the *RCL*) that belongs to the Epistle to the Hebrews and thus begins the semi-continuous sequence. Rather, the reason for its emphasis may be found in the causal phrases of the passage itself: "Therefore" . . . *because* "in these last days God has spoken to us by a Son, whom he appointed heir of all things" (1:1–2), and *because* this Son with his "powerful word" (1:3) is so far superior to the very angels or divine messengers (1:4–13) who have been "sent to serve of the sake of those who are to inherit salvation" (1:14), and *because* we are evidently in danger of drifting away from "what we have heard," which is the good—and "valid"!—news that "every transgression (and) disobedience (has) received a just penalty" in Christ Jesus our sinless high priest (4:15) who has offered his own blood (9:12; 13:12) in the Holy Place (9:2–26), and *because* we are evidently at risk of neglecting so great a salvation (2:3), in which case of neglect—according to the argument of Hebrews—there remains "no escape" from the punishment that we ourselves are not able to bear . . . therefore, . . . greater attention. Yes, the texts of Year D themselves will demand greater attention by virtue of the fact that they are often difficult. But the deeper necessity for greater attention is not cognitive or rationalistic; it is existential, it is eternal. The stakes literally could not be higher. *Therefore*, let the church run *no deficits* in this new attention-based economy. Let us never drift away from the gospel of Jesus Christ or neglect so great a salvation!

Acknowledgments

ANY VOLUME OF LITURGICAL ELEMENTS FOR CHRISTIAN WORSHIP IN THE Reformed tradition must necessarily begin and end and be permeated throughout with thanksgiving and praise to the Triune God. *Soli Deo Gloria!* But while the Trinity has also determined, by virtue of the grace of God's revelation, incarnation, mission, and covenantal nature, to involve and enlist many saints in the ongoing ministry of the Word and the Spirit, and while there are innumerable agents of God's grace for whom I do give thanks at this juncture, I will confine myself to mentioning those whose roles loom largest in my admittedly porous memory.

First of all, and most instrumentally, I give thanks for the two congregations I have been blessed to serve as pastor and interim pastor, respectively, for it is these congregations that first gave voice and lent their communal 'Amen' to these various elements, or something close to them: Central Presbyterian Church, Tarentum, PA (1995–2000) and First Presbyterian Church, Titusville, NJ (2004–2008). In the case of Year D, it was the latter congregation that served as its testing ground, and the fruits of it have been apparent.

The gracious pedagogical comments of the late Dr. Lucy Rose of Columbia Seminary continue to be instructive each time I teach worship. The prayers of the Rev. Roy Henderson at Lansdowne Parish Church, Glasgow, UK, a fine wordsmith, fed me for a year's worth of Sundays abroad, while the leaders of the Late Late Service, also in Glasgow, challenged me by example to think through the words used in worship with painstaking care (1992–93). Dr. Fred Anderson's labors at Madison Avenue Presbyterian Church and his enormous contribution to the worship of the Presbyterian Church (USA) are well documented, and I am grateful for the encouragement he has offered in our few, brief, but memorable exchanges.

The shape of Lavon Bayler's resources, *Taught By Love, Led By Love,* and *Gathered By Love* (United Church Press) which I ran across in 1996 and have used on occasion, inspired the notion that I might be able to build a similar resource over time, but in a more Reformed voice and vein.

Dr. Richard Young, now at Orchard Park Presbyterian Church in the Buffalo, NY, area, offered encouragement early on, and was a rare and delightful conversation partner as we were both serving in western PA.

My professors at Princeton Seminary, specifically, Dr. James F. Kay (now Dean), Dr. Sally Brown, and visiting lecturer Dr. Hughes Oliphant Old (now Dean of Erskine Seminary's Institute for Reformed Worship) prompted more critical (and self-critical) thinking about liturgical concerns, and I am grateful for their instruction in seminars, in their pedagogy, and in their scholarship.

I am also grateful to the First Presbyterian Church, Topeka, KS, which has served as my "safe home" sanctuary for going on fifty years. I am especially grateful to the long line of ministers, musicians, and other saints who have served that congregation over the years, and maintained a highly esthetic doxology; the Rev. C. Michael Kuner, who once served the church as both Associate Pastor and later as Interim Head of Staff, is my brother-in-law and has served as a mentor for many years; Mike's wife and my sister, Jennifer Kuner, has often filled the sanctuary with her exquisite solo (and choral) contributions, carrying on the contralto reverberations our mother first put in motion there beginning in the 1940s. My brother Rob and his wife Julie have always been encouraging where my writing is concerned, while my sisters Jen and Claire have rendered such care to our aging mother as has eased my own mind considerably, and freed me to labor at such projects as this one. Ashley Smith, of Cleveland, OH, a Presbyterian elder who works with the Cleveland Youth Orchestra, Karen Smith of Oakmont, PA, a frequent soprano soloist, and her mother (and Ashley's grandmother), the late Betty Hicks, a lifelong organist, joined in or initiated numerous discussions of worship through the years, and one is ever mindful of key considerations in light thereof. Of course, I am most grateful that the Lord saw fit to bring me into the world through, and place me in the care of, two of the most loving and gracious parents a child could ever hope for: my mother Dorothy Herrick Slemmons and my late father Robert Sheldon Slemmons. I continually give thanks, and I do so again now, that my parents raised us in the church: Sunday school, worship, youth choir, bell choir, youth group, etc., every week whenever each was in session.

Finally, I give thanks for Victoria, for whom worship is, not just in theory but in reality, the most joyous daily activity. She has graciously borne with me through the years in my labors on *Year D* and repeatedly confirmed its merits. I bless the Lord for her ministry of prayer, in song, and at the harp, for the sweetness of her voice and her spirit, and for the lovely sounds of her inspired psalm settings, to say nothing of all the other dimensions of the life of Christian marriage and friendship that we share in Christ. Nevertheless, *Come, Lord Jesus!*

PART I

The Christmas Cycle
Advent—Christmas—Epiphany

First Sunday of Advent

Malachi 1:1–14

Psalm 18

Luke 1:1–25

Hebrews 1:13—2:4

CALL TO WORSHIP

Call upon the LORD who is worthy to be praised!
For God is our stronghold, our shield, the horn of our salvation!
> The LORD hears the cries of his people.
> From his temple, God hears our cries of distress.
The LORD has bowed the heavens and come down!
He has reached down from on high and drawn us out of mighty waters.
> Lead us out, O God, into a broad place.
> For you have delivered a humble people.
It is you, O LORD, who light this lamp!
The LORD our God lights up our darkness!
> For this we extol you, O LORD, among the nations!
> We shall forever sing praises to your holy name!

OPENING PRAYER

Lord GOD of hosts, your name is great among the nations. From the rising of the sun to its setting, let your name be exalted, and let pure and worthy offerings be made to you. For you are the beloved of Jacob, great beyond the borders of Israel, and honor and respect are due you. Therefore, let our worship of your name be pure and pleasing to you. Look with favor upon us, take away our disgrace, let us hear and believe your holy Word, and do not let us fall silent concerning your Son, but give us courage to

3

tell the good news at home and abroad, that your people everywhere will return to you.

Call to Confession

Every transgression and every act of disobedience have received a just penalty! But how shall we escape if we neglect to own up to our need for God's justice, if we fail to grasp the enormity of God's grace in providing it or to consider what it cost the Son of God, who died to save us? Therefore, let us consider our sin and confess our need for this great salvation!

Prayer of Confession

O Lord our God, we confess that we have been slow to believe your promises, and quick to drift away from you. We have paid far too little attention to your word, to your testimony, to your miraculous signs and wonders, and far too much attention to selfish concerns. We have held back from you our very best, even though you gladly and graciously sent us your beloved and only begotten Son. Forgive us, O God, for our sinful thoughtlessness! Let us never again neglect so great a salvation as you have provided for us in Jesus Christ!

Declaration of Forgiveness

The LORD shows himself loyal to those who show themselves loyal, but with the crooked he shows himself perverse. The way of God is perfect. The promise of the LORD proves true. He is a rock for all who take refuge in him. You who have confessed and cried out to the LORD, know that you are delivered and forgiven, and be at peace.

Second Sunday of Advent

Numbers 12 OR 20:1–13 (14–21) 22–29

Psalm 106: (1) 7–18, 24–28 (43–48) (OR Psalm 95)

Luke 1: (57) 58–67 (68–79) 80

Hebrews 3:1–19

CALL TO WORSHIP

The LORD has raised up a horn for our salvation
in the house of his servant David!
**Blessed be the LORD, the God of Israel, for he has looked
with favor upon his people and redeemed them.**
Praise the LORD, who has shown us great mercy.
Prepare the way for the LORD our God!
Let the Holy Spirit descend, we pray!
Let the spirit of prophecy make us partners with Christ.
By the tender mercy of our God,
the dawn from on high will break upon us,
**to give light to those who sit in darkness and in the shadow of death,
to guide our feet into the way of peace.**

OPENING PRAYER

You, O God, are the builder of all things, and Christ Jesus, your Son, the faithful builder of your house, even as he serves as its head and cornerstone. Help us, O LORD, as partners with Christ, to be the house in which you dwell, that we may hold firm to faith and hope until the end, with boldness and unwavering confidence in you. Show your holiness, O God, to this assembly, among this people where your glory abides, in Jesus' name.

5

CALL TO CONFESSION

When our ancestors sojourned in the wilderness, they tested the LORD and rebelled against him, so that the Spirit said, "They always go astray in their hearts, and they have not known my ways," and that generation "will not enter my rest." Therefore, let not our hearts be hardened by the deceitfulness of sin, as on the day of rebellion, but let us, with believing hearts, confess our sin, seeking the mercy of God with our first confidence and with the pride that belongs to hope.

PRAYER OF CONFESSION

O LORD, you are good, and your steadfast love endures forever! Yet, we confess that though you have delivered us so many times, we are a disobedient and grumbling people, forgetful of your wonderful works, rebellious toward you, and by our own iniquity we are brought low. Nevertheless, O God, have regard for our distress. Remember your covenant of grace! Hear our cry, pity your captive people, show us your compassion, and deliver us from sin for your name's sake.

DECLARATION OF FORGIVENESS

The LORD has shown us the mercy he promised to our ancestors! He has remembered his holy covenant, the oath that he swore to Abraham and fulfilled with the gift of a mighty savior, giving knowledge of salvation by the forgiveness of our sins! Therefore, you who have been rescued and redeemed from your enemies and from the power of sin are free to serve the LORD in holiness and without fear, and to walk with him all of your days.

Third Sunday of Advent

Joshua 23:1–16

Psalm 81: (1) 2–9 (10–16) (OR Psalm 95)

Luke 3:23–38

Hebrews 4:1–11 (12–16)

CALL TO WORSHIP

The LORD has spoken and said:
"Let there be no strange god among you!"
> **But who has listened to the voice of the LORD?**
> **Are there any who have not bowed down to foreign gods?**
Yet, the LORD has promised to provide for you, saying,
"Open your mouth wide, and I will fill it!"
> **Our God is the LORD, who relieves us of our burdens,**
> **who has brought us up from the land of Egypt.**
Listen to the LORD! For his Sabbath rest remains open
to those who believe the promises of God.
> **Let us be united by faith as those who listen**
> **to the voice of the LORD, and walk in the light of his Word.**

OPENING PRAYER

O God, our strength, the God of Jacob, receive our songs and shouts of joy! Not for us, but for your name's sake, may our worship give you glory. Help us, we pray, that we might not fail to enter your rest, for we are weary of following our own ways and getting nowhere. Therefore, we seek you, knowing your reputation as our faithful provider, knowing your generosity and grace, that we might ask your blessings upon our land, our families, our children, and your church, that every onlooker might see and know that it is good to be near you and to trust in you as our God.

Call to Confession

No creature is hidden from God, but all are naked and laid bare to the eyes of the one to whom we must render an account. Yet, we have a great high priest who has passed through the heavens: Jesus, the Son of God, who is able to sympathize with our weaknesses. For he has been tested in every respect just as we are, yet he is without sin. Let us therefore approach the throne of grace with boldness, so that we may receive mercy and find grace to help in our time of need.

Prayer of Confession

Holy God, you are the Father of all the faithful, the Father of our Savior and Lord Jesus Christ. We confess, however, that we are weak and stubborn and slow to believe. Yet you, O God, offer us your strength! Give us the grace to be as humble as children and the courage to see ourselves in the light of your perfect goodness. In your mercy forgive us, and make us to be whom you want us to be—your Sabbath people, your family of faith, bound together by the love of your Son, the Lord of the Sabbath, in whose name we pray.

Declaration of Forgiveness

It is the LORD your God who has fought on your behalf, keeping your foes and enemies at bay. It is Christ Jesus himself, the Son of God, who has done all things well and fulfilled God's promise of a Savior. Therefore, hold fast to the LORD your God, and be very steadfast to observe and do all that he has commanded you, for by the grace of Jesus Christ we are forgiven and saved.

Fourth Sunday of Advent

Numbers 14:1–25

Psalm 144

John 3:22–38

Hebrews 5:11—6:20

CALL TO WORSHIP

Blessed be the LORD, my rock and my fortress,
my stronghold and my deliverer.
> Blessed be the LORD, my shield, in whom I take refuge,
> who subdues the peoples under the rule of his anointed one.

O LORD, what are human beings that you regard them,
or mortals that you consider them?
> They are like a breath, their days like a passing shadow.
> Yet, I will sing a new song to you, O God!

May the flock of the LORD increase by the thousands!
May there be no breach in our walls, no exiles, and no cry of distress.
> Happy are the people to whom such blessings fall!
> Happy are the people whose God is the LORD.

OPENING PRAYER

O LORD of heaven, come down! Let your lightning flash and scatter the darkness! Send out your arrows and rout your enemies. Stretch out your hand from on high, and set this people free from those who speak lies and those who love violence. For you, O LORD, are above all and your testimony is true! Your Son, whom you have sent, has spoken the words he has heard from you, our heavenly Father. May he give to each of us, and to your church, your Holy Spirit without measure.

9

Call to Confession

Surely, "The LORD is slow to anger, and abounding in steadfast love, forgiving iniquity and transgression." Yet just as surely our sins are not without consequence, for when God's people do not listen to his voice, submit to his word, or obey his Son, he gives them over to their stubborn hearts, to follow their own counsels; those who thus go their own way will not see life, but must endure God's wrath. Therefore, let us confess our iniquity to God and seek the LORD's forgiveness according to the greatness of his steadfast love, for he has pardoned his people, from Egypt even until now, and given us Jesus, a forerunner on our behalf, who has entered the holy place, having become our high priest forever.

Prayer of Confession

Righteous God, we confess that though we have heard your word many times and should be swift to obey you and to offer one another loving and gentle correction, we are often dull in our own understanding. We live as though unskilled in the word of righteousness. We are often forgetful and slow to practice the basic elements of the oracles of God. Forgive us, O LORD; raise us up into full maturity, that we might be well trained in your will and practiced in distinguishing good from evil. This we ask in Jesus' name.

Declaration of Forgiveness

The one who comes from heaven is above all. Whoever has accepted his testimony has certified this, that God is true. Whoever believes in the Son of God has eternal life; and we who have taken refuge in him have a great hope set before us, a sure and steadfast anchor of the soul: Jesus Christ, into whose hands God the Father, who loves him, has placed all things, never to be lost. Friends, be at peace. In Jesus Christ, you are forgiven.

Christmas Eve

Ecclesiastes 5:1–20 OR 7:1–14 OR Ezekiel 33:23–33

Psalm 21

Matthew 12:22–50 OR Luke 11:14–36 (37–54)

James 1:17–27

CALL TO WORSHIP

Guard your steps when you go to the house of God.
Draw near and listen!
> **Let us consider the work of God.**
> **Can anyone make straight what he has made crooked?**

God is in heaven, and you on the earth;
therefore let your words be few.
> **To draw near to listen is better than the sacrifice of fools;**
> **for they do not know how to keep from doing evil.**

But every good and perfect gift is from above,
coming down from the Father of lights,
eternal and unchanging, who gave us birth by the word of truth.
> **Therefore, let us welcome with meekness the implanted word,**
> **Jesus Christ, who has the power to save our souls!**
> **Be exalted, O LORD, in your strength!**
> **We will sing and praise your power.**

OPENING PRAYER

Holy and loving God, by your Holy Spirit, your Son Jesus Christ came to expose the darkness of this world, to cast out demons, to deal death to death, and to inaugurate your new heavenly reign in the midst of our languishing earthly reality. Christ Jesus, the only begotten, has declared that

11

everyone who does your will is his brother and sister, and he has blessed all who hear your word and obey it! Indeed, he himself is the Word of God. Help us, therefore, this night and always, to hear and receive him and all the good news concerning him, that we might forever be occupied with the true joy of hearts: Jesus Christ, the Son of David, who, being greater than Solomon, greater than Jonah, greater than all, is the Word and the wisdom that gives life!

Call to Confession

Jesus said, "On the day of judgment you will have to give an account for every careless word you utter; for by your words you will be justified, and by your words you will be condemned." Therefore, let us not be rash or quick to utter a word before God, but let us consider carefully how to rid ourselves of all forms of wickedness harbored in the human heart—anger, sordidness, greed, and deception—for out of the abundance of the heart the mouth speaks. And let us confess before God our need for a transformation of our hearts, that we might bring good things out of a good treasure and speak the Word of truth: the good news concerning the Son of God, Jesus Christ. Let us confess our sins and our need of Christ our Redeemer.

Prayer of Confession

Eternal God, holy and merciful, we confess that our speech has often led us into sin; our unbridled tongues have spoken words with which we have deceived ourselves and others; and our hearts have been so weighed down by worldly concerns that we have been blinded to the needs of others, neglectful of our responsibility for them, and forgetful of our accountability to you. We have often lived as though the gospel of your goodwill toward this world had never been heralded or heard. Forgive us, we pray, and cleanse us in spirit, soul, and body, both inside and out. Renew in us the gift of faith, that our faith may be pure and undefiled before you as we live in response to your grace, care for those in distress, and keep ourselves unstained by the world. Give us your Holy Spirit of mercy, charity, peace, and love, that we may be generous in speaking, in sharing, and in telling the joyful truth to all the world: the good news of Jesus Christ, your Son, our Savior and Lord, in whose holy name we pray.

Declaration of Forgiveness

Surely each day is a gift from God, and wisdom is a good inheritance. It is God alone who enables us to find enjoyment in life, who keeps us occupied with the joy of our hearts, and makes his children to be like good trees, bringing forth good fruit. This he does by the greatest gift of all, Christ Jesus, the word of truth implanted in our hearts and the Savior of our souls. Receive, therefore, the grace of God in Jesus Christ, believe the gospel, and be doers of the word, practicing the perfect law—the law not of death, but of freedom, liberty, and love. Know that in Jesus Christ you are forgiven, and be at peace.

Christmas Eve
A Festival of Lessons and Carols

A Festival of Lessons and Carols is a service that takes a considerable amount of coordinating with church musicians and readers. Modelled after the Festival of Nine Lessons and Carols, originally planned by Dean Eric Milner-White and first held on Christmas Eve 1918 at King's College, Cambridge, the following liturgy incorporates a number of fresh texts to complement the standard gospel lections, with the aim of recapitulating the narrative of salvation. Amidst all the other seasonal demands, coordinating such a service can often feel burdensome, and in the process of attending to many details, certain other ones can be easily overlooked. Even though the service traditionally relieves the preacher of the need to prepare a sermon, the preacher should think exegetically, attending to the following considerations in order to ensure that the service is decent, orderly, and coherent.

(1)   If there is a printed bulletin and the readings are listed therein, lectors should refrain from announcing the readings and from saying, "The Word of the Lord" after each reading. While this practice is otherwise appropriate, it is redundant and unnecessarily interrupts the overarching narrative in a service where there are nine lessons or more.

(2)   Indicate clearly when the people are to sit or stand, but do not ask the people to stand for every carol and sit for every reading. Group standing elements together, and sitting elements likewise. If you traditionally ask people to stand for the Gospel reading, then bear that in mind and group other standing (responsive) elements accordingly. Quieter carols are best sung while seated, whereas the more lively, joyful, and triumphant carols are best sung while standing. Although it is not always easy to arrange this while simultaneously

ensuring that readings and carol texts tell the story of redemption with a clear sense of progress and coherence, it remains a good general practice.

(3) Although the selection of carols may vary depending on the hymnal(s) and songbook(s) that are available to the people, those suggested here integrate with the readings in such a way as to recapitulate the story of salvation with coherence. So too can different Scripture selections be made so as to include other passages not traditionally read on Christmas Eve. Despite the unusual selections suggested in Year D, the traditional nativity narratives should not be overlooked or excluded.

(4) An old tradition provides for ordering the readers according to a certain ecclesial hierarchy, so that the first reader is a child or youth and the last is the "highest ranking" minister on hand. This approach is not recommended here, so as to avoid exalting the clergy or inverting the gospel's vision of the kingdom of heaven and the household of God.

(5) A significant, if not primary, aim of the service should be to ensure that those who attend only once or twice a year hear the gospel anew, and not merely in the same word-for-word fashion to which they may be accustomed. Several traditional readings are included here, but others are also included, notably the Romans and Hebrews texts, that frame the salvation history in a fresh way.

A Festival of Lessons and Carols

WORDS OF INTRODUCTION

Our worship service this night recounts the story of the birth of our Savior and Lord on the grand stage of salvation history—the whole drama, from Genesis to Revelation, of God's plan to redeem the cosmos, the nation of Israel, the church, and the individual from the powers of sin, death, and the devil. May you find it conducive to your worship of God, and may the Holy Spirit inspire you to ever greater joy, humility, and gratitude as you offer worship and adoration to him, our Wonderful Counselor, our Almighty God, our everlasting Father, and to Jesus Christ, our Prince of Peace. To God be the glory. Let us worship God.

*Prologue: 1 John 1:1–10

*Carol: "Let All Mortal Flesh Keep Silence"

*Bidding Prayer and the Lord's Prayer

Beloved of God in Christ, on this holy night, let us undertake to be reminded, to understand, and to delight in the great, mighty, and loving purpose of our holy and gracious God, from the first days of our primeval temptation, our fall, and our banishment from the Garden, to the final victory won for us by Jesus Christ, a victory that is foretold and promised in holy Scripture, and by all indications is coming soon to its fulfillment. Let us hear again the story of the incarnation of the Word of God, of the birth in Bethlehem of our glorious redeemer, Jesus Christ, who came to save. And let us ask the Lord to guide, quicken, and enliven our listening, by laying before him all concerns and offering him our full devotion and attention this night. Let us pray:

O Lord our God, surely it pleases you when we remember before you the needs of the whole world, especially the need for peace on earth and goodwill toward all people; the need for unity and love, for gentleness and fellowship, and all the fruits of the Spirit, within the church that your Son Jesus came to build, and especially here, in this congregation, in this denomination, and in all churches where you are sought.

Lord, we are reminded of the poor and the homeless, the cold, the hungry, the lonely, the sick, those who mourn, those whose relationships have suffered in this year that is passed and those whose faith has been sorely tested. We are reminded of the needs of the aged and the infirm, of the young and impressionable, and of those who care for one, the other, or both. Give rest to your weary servants, O Lord.

We pray as well for those who do not know you, for those who do not love you, and for all who have, by sin, grieved your loving heart.

Lastly, O Lord, we give you thanks for all who rejoice with us this night, but upon other shores—your church across the world—and especially those who rejoice in your presence on that heavenly shore, in a greater light, who no longer weep or suffer, who comprise that great multitude that no one can number, whose hope was in the Word made flesh, and with whom, in the Lord Jesus, we are forever and ever made one. These things we ask in the name of Jesus Christ, whose name is above all names, and who taught us to pray, saying:

Our Father . . .

*Carol: "Angels from the Realms of Glory"

First Lesson: Hosea 6:1–7

The Lighting of the Christ Candle

Second Lesson: Genesis 2:15–17; 3:4–6, 22–24

Third Lesson: Psalm 132

Carol: "Once in Royal David's City"

Fourth Lesson: Revelation 12:1–12, 17

Carol: "What Child Is This?"

Presentation of Tithes and Offerings

Offertory

*Doxology

*Prayer of Dedication
O Christ our King, you received gifts from the wise kings of old, and we would likewise offer you these gifts. May they be to you a fragrant offering, to bring healing and hope, relief and aid, to those in need, and may they be administered wisely, in accordance with your will.

*CAROL: "Good Christian Friends, Rejoice!"

FIFTH LESSON: Romans 5:12–21

CAROL: "See, Amid the Winter's Snow"

*SIXTH LESSON: Matthew 1:18–25

*CAROL: "O Little Town of Bethlehem"

*SEVENTH LESSON: Luke 2:8–20

CAROL: "Angels We Have Heard on High"

EIGHTH LESSON: Revelation 22:1–7, 10–21

*THE COLLECT FOR CHRISTMAS EVE

God of Hope, who sent Christ Jesus, our true light and our living hope, into this dark and dreary world for our forgiveness, our redemption, our reformation, and our joy, fill us now with all joy and peace in believing in him, so that we may abound in hope by the power of your Holy Spirit, for the glory of your name and for the completion of your godly joy; in Jesus' name.

*CAROL: "God Rest Ye Merry, Gentlemen"

*THE SHARING OF THE LIGHT OF CHRIST

*CAROL: "Silent Night, Holy Night"

*NINTH LESSON: Hebrews 1:1–4, 14; 2:1–3a

*THE BLESSING [Jude 24–25]

Now to him who is able to keep you from falling, and to make you stand without blemish in the presence of his glory with rejoicing, to the only God our Savior, through Jesus Christ our Lord, be glory, majesty, power, and authority, before all time and now and forever. Amen.

*POSTLUDE

Christmas Morning

Ecclesiastes 7:15–29 OR Micah 7:1–20

Psalm 44

Matthew 10:9–23 OR Luke 12:1–12

Romans 3:1–22a

CALL TO WORSHIP

Jesus said, "I tell you, everyone who acknowledges me before others,
the Son of Man also will acknowledge before the angels of God;
but whoever denies me before others
will be denied before the angels of God."

> **You are my King and my God;**
> **you have saved us from our foes;**
> **in you we have boasted continually,**
> **and we will give thanks to your name forever.**

"Whatever you have said in the dark will be heard in the light,
and what you have whispered behind closed doors
will be proclaimed from the housetops."

> **We have heard with our ears, O God, our ancestors have told us**
> **of the deeds you performed in their days, in the days of old.**
> **Rouse yourself! Why do you sleep, O LORD?**
> **Awake, do not cast us off forever!**

"Are not five sparrows sold for two pennies?
Yet not one of them is forgotten in God's sight.
But even the hairs of your head are all counted.
Do not be afraid; you are of more value than many sparrows."

> **Rise up, O LORD, and come to our help.**
> **Redeem us for the sake of your steadfast love.**

Let not your righteous perish in righteousness,
or the wicked prosper in evildoing.
Let us not spend our days in vanity.

Opening Prayer

O Holy Savior, Son of God and Son of David, shepherd your people
with your staff, as in the days of old, the flock that belongs to you, which
abides in the midst of a garden land; show us marvelous things, as in the
days when you came out of Egypt, so that the nations shall see, cover
their mouths, and be ashamed of all their might. For you came into this
world with nothing, and you have called us to go forth with nothing but
your Spirit to teach us what to say, speaking peace to those who receive
you and remaining at peace in the face of rejection. Give us, therefore,
strength and sustenance for this earthly life, that we may have hope and
courage to endure, for you have promised that those who endure to the
end will be saved.

Call to Confession

Surely there is no one on earth so righteous as to do good without ever
sinning. For though God made human beings straightforward, he knows
the secrets of the heart, and how inclined it is to devise many schemes.
Truly, nothing is covered up that will not be uncovered, and nothing is secret that will not become known. For all are under the power of sin: There
is no one who is righteous, not even one; all have turned aside; there is no
one who shows kindness; there is no fear of God before their eyes. Truly,
the faithful have disappeared from the land, and there is no one left who is
upright; but the whole world will be held accountable to God. Therefore,
let us repudiate sin and confess our need of our forgiving and redeeming
Savior, Jesus Christ, born to save, now in our midst, and coming again.

Prayer of Confession

O LORD, God of our salvation, who is like you, pardoning iniquity
and passing over the transgression of the remnant of your possession?
For you have shown faithfulness to Jacob and unswerving loyalty to
Abraham, as you swore to our ancestors from the days of old. We confess that we have not been true to your covenant; we have not always
welcomed your prophecies and your prophets, nor have we obeyed your

Word, your only begotten Son; we have allowed worldly desires to distract us from your will; and we have resisted the reign that Jesus came to preach, establish, and fulfill. Forgive us, heavenly Father, for every sinful thought, every careless word, and every sinful deed, whether of action or inaction. Have mercy, O Lord; cast all our sins into the depths of the sea. Bring us out from our darkness and into the light of your Son, that we may see and rejoice in his vindication and glory. This we ask, confident that your faithfulness is greater than our faithlessness, certain that, even if everyone is a liar, you will be proven true!

Declaration of Forgiveness

The Lord does not retain his anger forever, but delights in showing clemency. Forgiving, gracious, and compassionate, he hears the cries of those who wait for the God of salvation. If for a time we have borne the indignation of our Lord, he will soon execute judgment on our behalf, establishing his people, setting us free, delighting in us, and commanding our victory. For now, apart from the law, the righteousness of God has been revealed through faith in Jesus Christ for all who believe in him. As for those who are in Christ: though we may fall, we shall rise again. Therefore, I declare to you in the name of Jesus Christ, you are redeemed, forgiven, and free.

Christmas Day

Isaiah 6:8–13 OR Jeremiah 10:1–16 (17–25)

Psalm 35 OR Psalm 94

John 12:17–19, 37–50

Romans 11:2(b)–28 (29–32) 33–36

CALL TO WORSHIP

The gods who did not make the heavens and the earth
shall perish from the earth and from under the heavens.
>   **They are both stupid and foolish;**
>   **the instruction given by idols is no better than wood!**
>   **They are worthless, a work of delusion;**
>   **at the time of their punishment they shall perish.**
Not like these is the LORD, for the LORD is the true God;
he it was who formed all things, the living God and the everlasting King.
>   **At his wrath the earth quakes;**
>   **the nations cannot endure his indignation.**
It was he who made the earth by his power,
who established the world by his wisdom
and by his understanding stretched out the heavens.
>   **When he utters his voice, there is a tumult of waters in the heavens;**
>   **he makes lightning for the rain**
>   **and summons wind from his storehouses;**
>   **he makes the mist rise from the ends of the earth.**
>   **The LORD of hosts is his name!**

Opening Prayer

There is none like you, O Lord, whose name is mighty and powerful. Who would not fear you, O King of the nations? For that is your due. Among all the wise ones of the nations and in all their kingdoms there is no one like you, who have sent your Son, Jesus Christ, as light into the world, that everyone who believes in him should not remain in darkness. For whoever sees and believes in the Son sees and believes in you, our heavenly Father. Grant us, therefore, by the gift of your Holy Spirit, the light to see you clearly and the faith to believe in you fully, that we might testify to your truth and your love, for the service of your glory and for the sake of those lost in sin, crippled by fear, and weighed down by the cares of this world.

Call to Confession

The Lord knows our thoughts, that they are but an empty breath. He who planted the ear, does he not hear? He who formed the eye, does he not see? He who disciplines the nations, he who teaches knowledge to humankind, does he not chastise? As Jesus has said, "The one who rejects me and does not receive my word has a judge; on the last day the word that I have spoken will serve as judge." Yet he gives them respite from trouble; they are counted happy and blessed who welcome his discipline, for the Lord will not forsake his people; he will not abandon his heritage. Let us, therefore, in penitence and faith, confess our sins to God, who banishes ungodliness and takes away sins.

Prayer of Confession

Remember, O Lord, what your prophet has said, that the way of human beings is not in their control, that mortals as they walk cannot direct their steps. Remember, O Lord, and have mercy. Correct your children, O Lord, but in just measure; not in your anger, or you will bring us to nothing. For we confess not only our sins and misdeeds; we confess that, although you have performed countless signs in our presence, we have not always believed in your power, trusted in your grace, or remembered your mercies toward us; and when we have believed in you, we have often let the fear of human opinion keep us from testifying to your grace and glory. Forgive us, O Lord, for every sin we have committed, every affront we have caused; set us free from every illicit or frustrating bond; liberate your people for new life, as was and is your intended purpose in sending your Son Jesus Christ in the flesh to redeem us.

Declaration of Forgiveness

Shout for joy and be glad; say evermore, "Great is the Lord, who delights in the welfare of his servants." Let those whom Christ has redeemed tell of his righteousness and praise the Lord all day long. For God has commanded eternal life for all who believe in Christ Jesus, who said, "I came not to judge the world, but to save the world." Therefore, let us rejoice in the Lord, exult in his deliverance, and give thanks forevermore that in Jesus Christ we are forgiven.

First Sunday after Christmas

Genesis 14:1–24

Psalm 110

Matthew 8:14–34 OR Mark 5:1–20

Hebrews 7:1–28

CALL TO WORSHIP

Blessed be the God Most High, maker of heaven and earth,
>   **who has delivered his enemies**
>   **into the hand of his servant.**
Blessed be the God and Father of our Lord Jesus Christ,
>   **who has said to his only begotten Son,**
>   **"Sit at my right hand until I make your enemies your footstool."**
Come and worship the LORD, who has sent out his mighty scepter.
>   **Rule in the midst of your foes, O Son of David!**
>   **For we offer ourselves willingly to you, our High Priest and King!**

OPENING PRAYER

Lord Jesus Christ, the Son of God and Son of Man, you came to heal the sick, to drive out demons, to take our infirmities and bear our diseases, yet you had no place to lay your head. You, our sinless Savior and Lord, are the guarantee of a better covenant than the old priesthood was able to provide. Therefore, we thank you for your tireless ministry on our behalf, for your humble way of coming among us, for your grace even in the face of rejection by those whom you came to seek, to serve, and to save. Thank you that we can receive you anew today, and be made ready for that day when we shall see you face to face.

CALL TO CONFESSION

Christ Jesus holds his priesthood permanently, because of his eternal nature. Consequently, he is able for all time to save those who approach God through him, since he always lives to make intercession for them. God has deemed it right and fitting that we should have such a high priest, holy, blameless, undefiled, set apart from sin, and exalted above the heavens. Therefore, by all means let us call upon him to do for us what he was appointed to do, that which we cannot do for ourselves. Let us confess our sin and our need of him.

PRAYER OF CONFESSION

O Christ our Savior, yours is the power of an indestructible life! Yet we are mortal, compromised by sin, easily distracted from devotion to you, easily attracted by and accommodated to the surrounding culture. Saving Lord, save us from ourselves, and from every sinful thing that would come between us and you. Cut off every path of retreat from you, that as you draw us to yourself, we would not draw back, but lean into your presence, enter your rest, and learn to enjoy eternal fellowship with you, our true King of Peace, our true King of Righteousness!

DECLARATION OF FORGIVENESS

The Lord is fully able, fully willing to forgive, and is quick to do so; before the sincere and contrite of heart have finished speaking, it is done. He is able to command even the wind and the sea, and they obey him. Therefore, let the inner storms of anxiety and guilt, of fear and doubt, be silenced. For by virtue of the unending priestly ministry of Jesus Christ, you are forgiven. Henceforth, live into that forgiveness—let your faith be strong, your hope large, your devotion true, and let a new resolve be born in your heart to walk in the ways of holiness, purity, righteousness, and peace.

Second Sunday after Christmas

Exodus 25:1–40

Psalm 73

Matthew 11: (1–11) 12–24 (25–30) OR Luke 7:18–35

Hebrews 8:1–13

CALL TO WORSHIP

My flesh and my heart may fail,
but God is the strength of my heart and my portion forever.
> May our worship of God on earth
> reflect the true worship of God in heaven.
Thank you, Father, Lord of heaven and earth,
for you have hidden your truth from the wise and the intelligent.
> Yet you have revealed it to infants!
> Yes, Father, for such was your gracious will!
Come to Jesus, all you who are weary and are carrying heavy burdens,
and he will give you rest. Take his yoke upon you, and learn from him.
> For our Lord is gentle and humble in heart, offering rest for the soul,
> a yoke that is easy, and a burden that is light.

OPENING PRAYER

Blessed and Holy God, where but in your sanctuary can we see the world so clearly? When can we understand ourselves better than when we stand in your almighty and merciful presence? Give us, O LORD, faith to see what eyes cannot see, and a heart to hear what ears alone cannot discern! Attune our spirits to your Spirit moving among and ministering to us, even as we offer you what devotion, worship, love, and service are due you.

Call to Confession

We have such a high priest, one who is seated at the right hand of the throne of the Majesty in the heavens, a minister in the sanctuary and the true tent that the Lord, and not any mere mortal, has set up. Jesus, the mediator of a better covenant, enacted through better promises, has obtained the most excellent ministry, of which God has said, "I will put my laws in their minds, and write them on their hearts, and I will be their God, and they shall be my people. And they shall not teach one another or say to each other, 'Know the Lord,' for they shall all know me, from the least of them to the greatest. For I will be merciful toward their iniquities, and I will remember their sins no more." Therefore, let us approach God through Christ Jesus, the High Priest of the new covenant.

Prayer of Confession

Our holy and gracious God, truly you are good to the upright, to those who are pure in heart. But we confess that we have harbored envy, pride, and bitterness in our hearts. We have seen how the wicked seem to prosper, at least for a time, yet we have often failed to see the slippery slopes on which you have placed them. Forgive us, O God, for our foolishness, for our ignorance and blindness, for desiring things that are contrary to your will, for being untrue to the circle of your children. For there is nothing on earth worth desiring above you, and we have no hope of heaven apart from you. Forgive us, O God, and lead us ever more deeply into your will, for it is good for us to be near you, and to have Christ Jesus, your Son, as our refuge.

Declaration of Forgiveness

Though sin has at times made us senseless, thoughtless, and unfeeling toward God, still the Lord has promised to be with us until the end of the age. Truly, the Lord is near. Even now, he reaches out to you, offers to hold you and lead you by the hand. Therefore, let the Lord forever guide you with the wise counsel of his Word and sustain you with his Holy Spirit, for though he will put an end to all falsehood, afterward he will receive you with honor.

Epiphany

Deuteronomy 4:9–24 (25–31) 32–40

Psalm 75 OR Psalm 76

1 John 2:3–29

John 5:31–47

CALL TO WORSHIP

Glorious are you, O LORD our God,
more majestic than the everlasting mountains!
> **You, O LORD, are awesome indeed!**
> **Who can stand before you when your anger is aroused?**
God is known in the land of Judah, his name is great in Israel.
For the LORD our God is a jealous God, a holy God, a devouring fire.
> **His abode is Jerusalem, Zion his dwelling place.**
> **But what god has ever taken a nation for himself**
> **as the LORD our God has done?**
Acknowledge today and take to heart that the LORD is God,
in heaven above and on the earth beneath; there is no other!
> **Let us assemble and hear the words of the LORD,**
> **that we may fear him as long as we live,**
> **and teach our children to do so!**

OPENING PRAYER

Glory be to you, eternal God, to you who were from the beginning and
who shall ever be! For the darkness of the world is passing away and your
true light is already shining. You, who have spoken through your prophets, inspired the Scriptures, testified to your Son and empowered him to
do your mighty works of love; you, the Father of our Lord Jesus Christ,

whom we confess as the Truth and the Light of the world—you will surely bring your love to perfection in those who obey you! Therefore, help us, Almighty God, to abide in you, to walk just as Christ Jesus has walked, to be born of your Holy Spirit, and to come to you for eternal life! For this is why Jesus Christ has come, and we ask this in his holy name.

CALL TO CONFESSION

The LORD scatters those who serve gods made by human hands, objects of wood and stone that neither see, nor hear, nor eat, nor smell. But if you will seek the LORD your God, and search after him with all your heart and soul, you will find him. Therefore, let sinners return to the LORD. Let them heed and obey him. For the LORD your God is a merciful God; he will neither abandon nor destroy those who seek him, and he will not forget the covenant that he made with our ancestors in the faith. Therefore, let us seek the LORD together in the confession of our sins.

PRAYER OF CONFESSION

O God our Father, we confess that we have loved and fed the desire of the flesh, the desire of the eyes, and the pride of riches, which come not from you, but from the world of sin. Yet, as you have shown us, the world and its desire are passing away, while those who love you, who love your Son, who abide in you and do your will, shall live forever. We acknowledge that Christ Jesus your Son is altogether righteous, even as we confess our need of him. Forgive us, Holy One, for our former, false, and sinful ways, and take away from us every cause for stumbling. Anoint us with the Spirit of the LORD, and let your anointing and your true teaching abide in us, along with the saving knowledge of our Lord Jesus Christ.

DECLARATION OF FORGIVENESS

Let the Word that you have heard from the beginning abide in you! For this is the good news: If what you heard from the beginning abides in you, then you will abide in the Son and in the Father. As the word of God abides in you, your sins are forgiven on account of his name, and you have overcome the evil one. Therefore, receive the Spirit of the Lord, who has promised you eternal life. Know that you are forgiven, and be at peace.

PRESENTATION OF TITHES AND OFFERINGS

Make vows to the LORD your God, and perform them! Let all who are around him bring gifts to the Awesome One, who breaks the spirit of the rulers of the world, who inspires fear in the kings of the earth. Let us present unto God our tithes and offerings, and thereby give him glory.

First Sunday after Epiphany
Ordinary Time 1 (*Baptism of the Lord*)

Leviticus 16:1–34

Psalm 69

Matthew 14:1–12

Hebrews 9:1–28

CALL TO WORSHIP [Psalm 69:30–36]

I will praise the name of God with a song;
I will magnify him with thanksgiving.
> **This will please the LORD more than an ox**
> **or a bull with horns and hoofs.**

Let the oppressed see it and be glad;
you who seek God, let your hearts revive!
> **For the LORD hears the needy,**
> **and does not despise his own that are in bonds.**

Let heaven and earth praise him,
the seas and everything that moves in them.
> **For God will save Zion**
> **and rebuild the cities of Judah;**
> **and his servants shall live there and possess it;**

the children of his servants shall inherit it,
> **and those who love his name shall live in it.**

OPENING PRAYER

LORD God of Hosts, in whose beloved Son Jesus Christ we are joined together through the one baptism, begun in the Jordan and completed on the cross, draw near and refresh us with your presence, restore us to the joy of your salvation, for our prayer is to you alone, O Lord. May this be an acceptable time, O God, for you speak to us and answer us in the abundance of your steadfast love, for though we are yours through the waters of regeneration, yet there remain many forces in this world that threaten to overwhelm and swallow us up. Do not hide your face from your servants in distress, but reveal yourself and make haste to answer us; with your faithful help rescue us, for we sink in the mire of this dying world. Draw near and redeem your people; set us free from every enemy, every entrapment, every temptation, and every snare. Deliver us from the deep waters into the new life that Christ alone offers, who is at once the Lamb of God and the High Priest of the new and better and everlasting covenant. This we ask in Jesus' name.

Call to Confession

Through the ancient rituals of Israel, the Holy Spirit has revealed but an earthly sketch of the heavenly worship that, Scripture says, only the better sacrifice, the blood of Jesus Christ himself, could set right. For not even the first covenant was inaugurated without blood; indeed, under the old law, almost everything was purified with blood, for without the shedding of blood there is no forgiveness of sins. Yet Christ Jesus did not enter a sanctuary made by human hands, a mere copy of the true one, but he entered into heaven itself, to appear in the presence of God on our behalf. Nor was it to offer himself again and again, as the high priest would do year after year with blood that was not his own; for then he would have had to suffer again and again since the foundation of the world. But as it is, he has appeared once for all at the end of the age to remove sin by the sacrifice of himself. And just as it is appointed for mortals to die once, and after that the judgment, so Christ, having been offered once to bear the sins of many, will appear a second time, not to deal with sin, but to save those who are eagerly waiting for him. Friends, since we have such a gracious, self-sacrificing high priest, let us confess our sins, that we may escape the coming judgment and be free to regard his second coming eagerly and without fear.

Prayer of Confession

O God, you know our folly, and the wrongs we have done are not hidden from you. We confess our sins and we stand in need of your forgiveness

and mercy. Do not let the flood of our transgressions sweep over us, or the depth of our uncleanness swallow us up. But let the holy ministry of your Son and his once-for-all atonement for sins effect our salvation according to your grace. Answer us, O Lord, for your steadfast love is good. According to your abundant mercy, turn to us and forgive us. Do not let those who hope in you be put to shame because of our sins, O Lord God of hosts, nor let those who seek you be dishonored because of the failings of your people. Help us bear credible, winsome, and joyful witness to the loving truth and redeeming grace of Jesus Christ in the midst of this lost and violent generation; this we ask for the honor and glory of his name.

DECLARATION OF FORGIVENESS

Friends, hear the saving gospel of Jesus Christ, who, when he came as high priest of the good things to come, entered once for all into the Holy Place, not with the blood of bulls and goats, but with his own blood, thus obtaining eternal redemption. For if the blood of goats and bulls, with the sprinkling of the ashes of a heifer, once sanctified those who were defiled so that their flesh was purified, how much more will the blood of Christ, who through the eternal Spirit offered himself without blemish to God, purify our conscience from dead works to worship the living God! For this reason he is the mediator of a new covenant, so that those who are called may receive the promised eternal inheritance, because a death has occurred that redeems us from our transgressions under the first covenant. Therefore, believe the good news: In Jesus Christ we are forgiven, and free to receive eternal life, eternal redemption, an eternal inheritance, and eternal peace. Thanks be to God!

Second Sunday after Epiphany
Ordinary Time 2

Isaiah 26:7–27:1

Psalm 109

Hebrews 10:1–4, 10–14, 26–39

Matthew 8:1–4; 9:1–8 OR Luke 5:12–26

CALL TO WORSHIP

The way of the righteous is level, O merciful God of justice!
You make smooth the path of the righteous.
> **In the path of your judgments, O LORD, we wait for you;**
> **your name and your renown are the soul's desire.**
My soul yearns for you in the night,
my spirit within me earnestly seeks you.
> **For when your judgments are in the earth,**
> **the inhabitants of the world learn righteousness.**
Your hand, O LORD, is lifted up, but the wicked do not see it.
Let them see your zeal for your people!
> **For you, O LORD, ordain peace for us;**
> **indeed, all that we have done, you have done for us.**

OPENING PRAYER

Holy and merciful God, to whom alone vengeance belongs, who alone is trustworthy to administer it rightly: we thank you that Christ Jesus your Son has borne the punishment for our sins, thereby providing for us a narrow way into a broad space through the offering of his body, once for all, an offering by which we have been and are being sanctified. Therefore, let the name of Jesus be exalted! For he is worthy of praise who is seated at your right hand, awaiting the day when all his enemies will be a footstool for his feet. May his atoning work secure the hearts of all who belong to you through his single sacrifice for sins, the sacrifice he has made so as to perfect for all time those who are being refined and rendered holy by the gracious work of your Spirit!

CALL TO CONFESSION

If we willfully persist in sin after having received the knowledge of the truth, there no longer remains a sacrifice for sins, but a fearful prospect of judgment, and a fury of fire that will consume God's adversaries. How much worse will it be for those who spurn the Son of God and outrage the Spirit of grace? It is a fearful thing to fall into the hands of the living God. But for those who show endurance, who do not shrink back but remain confident in God's mercy, there is promised a great reward. The way of the righteous is the way of faith, and it demands that we be honest with God and honest with ourselves about our sins and our need of grace. Therefore, let us acknowledge the holiness of God and our need for forgiveness in Christ.

PRAYER OF CONFESSION

O LORD our God, we confess that other lords besides you have ruled over us, but we acknowledge your name alone. For you stand at the right hand of the needy, to save them from those who would condemn them to death. And we ourselves are among them as those who stand in absolute need of you—you who have the power to heal, you who have the power to make us clean. Therefore help us, O LORD; come quickly to our aid! Save us from the power of sin, according to your steadfast love. Then let the world see the gracious favor you have shown us and know that it is your hand at work in us—that you, O LORD, have done it. For we will give great thanks to you and praise you in the midst of the great congregation! This we ask in Jesus' name.

DECLARATION OF FORGIVENESS

Hear the gospel of our Lord Jesus Christ, who has come with authority to forgive sins, and with power to perform miracles so as to confirm the good news of forgiveness: In a very little while, the one who is coming will come and will not delay; and those who have been made righteous in him will live by faith. Therefore, have faith. Let nothing cause you to shrink back and so be lost, but have confidence in God, and stand firm among those who share faith in the Lord and so are saved. For in Jesus Christ, we are forgiven.

Third Sunday after Epiphany
Ordinary Time 3

Job 32:1–22

Psalm 89:5–18; 38–52

Hebrews 11: (1–3) 4–7, 17–28 (39–40)

Luke 5:27–39

CALL TO WORSHIP

Let the heavens praise your wonders, O LORD,
your faithfulness in the assembly of the holy ones!
> **For who in the skies can be compared to the LORD?**
> **Who among the heavenly beings is like the LORD?**

The LORD is a God feared in the council of the holy ones,
great and awesome above all that are around him!
> **O LORD God of hosts, who is as mighty as you?**
> **Your faithfulness, O LORD, surrounds you!**

Happy are the people who know the festal shout,
who walk, O LORD, in the light of your countenance!
> **Blessed be the LORD forever! Amen and Amen.**

OPENING PRAYER

O LORD, our faithful God, your Word has revealed that without faith it is impossible to please you, for whoever would approach you must believe that you exist and that you reward those who seek you! Therefore, we have come, trusting that you do indeed exist, expecting you to meet us here, and seeking your face, the face of our Invisible God, as though you were indeed visible. For in Christ Jesus, you have in fact become fully human and revealed to us your true nature. Therefore, anything that we might suffer for the sake of Christ, who has suffered for us, is surely a greater reward than all the treasures of Egypt! Come, O LORD, and make us complete! Bring the good work you have begun in us to perfection!

CALL TO CONFESSION

When the scribes and the Pharisees asked, "Why do you eat and drink with tax collectors and sinners?" Jesus answered, "Those who are well have no need of a physician, but those who are sick. I have come to call not the righteous but sinners to repentance." Therefore, let every sinner who would sit at table with our Lord confess and renounce sin, and seek the forgiveness, the grace, and the healing that our divine physician alone can give.

PRAYER OF CONFESSION

Remember, O LORD, how short our time is—for what vanity you have created all flesh! Who can live and never see death? Who among the living has not sinned against you? Yet surely we are without excuse. Neither can we find safety in numbers. We confess that each of us has sinned in thought, word, and deed, transgressed your laws and failed to fulfill your commandments. Forgive us, O LORD, for the sake of your steadfast love of old, your faithfulness that you swore to our ancestors. Remember, O LORD, how you sent your Son, Christ Jesus, to heal and save on his mission of reconciliation, so that he himself has become for us the gospel of forgiveness and new life. Let his purpose and mission be fulfilled in our lives this very day, by the transforming grace of your everlasting mercy.

DECLARATION OF FORGIVENESS

Surely our shield belongs to the LORD, to Christ our King, the Holy One of Israel! For he himself, the LORD's anointed, was spurned, scorned, and rejected, enduring God's wrath as it was poured out upon him as the punishment for our sin. Jesus himself saw the days of his youth cut short for our sake; Christ our Savior was covered with the shame that we deserved. In this is grace, the grace by which we are saved, that the immortal God, who is able to raise someone from the dead, has himself died and been raised, and he calls us to follow him into everlasting life. This he has done for the very purpose of our avoiding destruction and being brought, instead, to perfection with all the saints. Therefore, in the good faith that belongs to righteousness, receive the unmerited approval of God, and do not surrender the hope and the conviction that will keep you on the way to life!

Fourth Sunday after Epiphany
Ordinary Time 4

Job 33:1–33

Psalm 34:11–18

Matthew 12:1–21 OR Mark 3:7–19 OR Luke 6:1–16

Hebrews 12: (1–3) 4–17

CALL TO WORSHIP

Come, O children, listen to me.
I will teach you the fear of the LORD.
> **For God speaks in one way, and in two,**
> **though people do not perceive it.**
In a dream, in a vision of the night,
he opens their ears, and terrifies them with warnings.
> **Thus, the LORD calls us away from evil deeds,**
> **and would keep us from the sin of pride.**
Which of you desires life, and covets many days to enjoy good?
Keep your tongue from evil, and your lips from speaking deceit.
> **Pursue peace with everyone, seek peace and pursue it,**
> **along with holiness, without which no one will see the LORD!**

OPENING PRAYER

Praise be to you, O Lord of the Sabbath, for you have made the Sabbath for our sake, taking into account our need for refreshment, renewal, and rest! Yet you have also called us to be disciplined, and you discipline those whom you love and chastise every child whom you accept. Thank you, Lord, that even your discipline, though it may seem painful rather than pleasant at the time, is a sign of your love and acceptance. Therefore, come! Receive our praise and teach us! Grant each of us a teachable spirit, that we would now concern ourselves not with advising or correcting our neighbors, but with listening to your voice speaking to our own particular need. Instruct and inspire us, correct and admonish us, that we may share in your holiness and trust in the knowledge that you discipline us only for our good.

Call to Confession

The eyes of the LORD are on the righteous, and his ears are open to their cry. But the face of the LORD is against evildoers, to cut off the remembrance of them from the earth. When the righteous cry for help, the LORD hears, and rescues them from all their troubles. The LORD is near to the brokenhearted and saves the crushed in spirit. Therefore, let not your heart be unbroken by the effect of sin upon your own life, and let not your spirit carry on unchecked by the damage sin and evil have done in your own relationship with God and with his people. But let us confess our sin and avail ourselves of the rescue that God extends to those who call upon him for mercy.

Prayer of Confession

Holy, healing Lord, you who desire mercy and not sacrifice, we confess we have too rarely shown mercy to others, and too often condemned the guiltless. We have allowed sin to cling to us rather than cast it aside. We have at times regarded your discipline far too lightly, and at other times given in to discouragement when we felt the sting of rebuke. We have allowed the root of bitterness and defilement to grow among us. But let it now be uprooted! Cleanse and heal us, renew and restore us, O God. Let us never forget that you love us with the holy love of a father, and that you intend every word of discipline for our growth and improvement. Forgive us thoroughly, make our sins whiter than snow, and give us courage to live once again and forever in the light of your countenance.

Declaration of Forgiveness

Look to Jesus, the pioneer and perfecter of our faith, who, for the sake of the joy set before him, has endured the cross, disregarding its shame, and taken his seat at the right hand of the throne of God. His joy is the joy of a giver who knows that his gift is precisely what is needed: for God, the vindication of holiness, and for the sinner, the gift of salvation, redemption, and the purification of sins. Therefore, let the forgiving, atoning work of Christ clear the ground in your life for peace and righteousness to grow as you are trained by them, and do not be afraid to endure trials for the sake of discipline, for in Christ Jesus, the Son of God, the Father is treating you too as his children, so that you may share in his holiness.

Fifth Sunday after Epiphany
Ordinary Time 5

Job 34:1–20

Psalm 28

Matthew 6:7–15

Hebrews 13:9–14 (15–16) 17–25

CALL TO WORSHIP

If the LORD should take back his spirit to himself,
and gather to himself his breath,
> **all flesh would perish together,**
> **and all mortals return to dust.**
Blessed be the LORD, for he hears the pleas of his people!
The LORD is my strength and my shield; in him my heart trusts!
> **So I am helped, and my heart exults,**
> **and with my song I give thanks to him.**
The LORD is the strength of his people;
he is the saving refuge of his anointed.
> **O save your people, and bless your heritage!**
> **Be our shepherd and our guide forever!**

OPENING PRAYER

O God our Father, your Son and our Lord Jesus Christ is the same yester-
day and today and forever. We realize, in light of the constant changes and
challenges we face, that we have no lasting city here on earth, but we look
for the city, the new Jerusalem, that is to come. Through your Son and in
his Spirit, we offer you our continual sacrifice of praise, the fruit of those
who confess his name. Accept, then, our songs and prayers of praise and

45

adoration, and strengthen our hearts with grace, for we seek the bread of your presence, and we gather at the table where your Son has offered the blood of the eternal covenant, in whose name we pray.

CALL TO CONFESSION

Jesus' instructions regarding prayer include the regular and disciplined request for forgiveness, along with the presupposition that the forgiveness we hope to receive stands in direct proportion to the thoroughness with which we forgive others. We therefore confess our sins, seek forgiveness, and renounce all condemnation of others.

PRAYER OF CONFESSION

Holy God, righteous and mighty, you love justice and repay to all according to their work. We ourselves can claim no innocence in your presence, neither have we paid sufficient regard to your works of power and love. Hear the sound of our pleadings, O Lord, for we are broken down and longing to be built up once more. Bring to our minds every sin that has yet to be confessed or forgiven, that we might take action to make peace and be reconciled to our neighbors, and say to you without any trace of hypocrisy: "Forgive us our debts, as we also have forgiven our debtors." Cleanse us of every stain, grant us the gracious gift of a clear conscience, and instill in us the earnest desire to act honorably in all things. This we ask in Jesus' holy and exalted name.

DECLARATION OF FORGIVENESS

Hear the good news: As Jesus suffered outside the city gate in order to sanctify his people by his own blood, we likewise have no lasting city here, but we look for the city that is to come. Henceforth, we are free to walk with him who gave his life for us—free to live unafraid, do good deeds, and share with others what we have been given. Through Christ, therefore, let us continually offer a sacrifice of praise to God, that is, the fruit of lips that confess his name. For in Jesus Christ, we are forgiven.

BENEDICTION [Hebrews 13:20–21]

Now may the God of peace, who brought back from the dead our Lord Jesus, the great shepherd of the sheep, by the blood of the eternal covenant, make you complete in everything good so that you may do his will, working among us that which is pleasing in his sight, through Jesus Christ, to whom be the glory forever and ever. Amen.

Sixth Sunday after Epiphany / Proper 1
Ordinary Time 6

Job 34:21–37

Psalm 12

Matthew 7:1–12

2 Peter 1:1–15

CALL TO WORSHIP

Jesus said, "Do not give what is holy to dogs;
and do not throw your pearls before swine.
> **For they will trample them under foot**
> **and turn and maul you."**
But direct your worship to the living God,
whose promises are pure and who fulfills them perfectly.
> **You, O Lord, will protect us;**
> **you will guard us from this generation forever!**
Come, you for whom entry into the eternal kingdom of Jesus Christ
has been richly provided.
> **Amen! Let us confirm our call and election.**
> **Let us worship the Lord, the living and true God!**

OPENING PRAYER

Heavenly Father, who gives far greater gifts, and far more readily, than
even the best of human parents, through your Son Jesus Christ you have
taught us to direct our petitions and requests to you, asking, searching,
and knocking for access to you and to your kingdom. Grant us, we pray,
the greatest gift, your holy presence among us, and one thing more: the
good sense to recognize that you are among us, to harbor a spirit of

gratitude and joy, to trust in your gracious Spirit for everything we need, and to believe in your perfect promises—all of this, even though we live in the midst of such a generation! In Jesus' name we pray.

CALL TO CONFESSION

The eyes of God are upon the ways of mortals, and he sees all their steps. There is no gloom or deep darkness where evildoers may hide themselves. But all human vision is obscured and inverted, for people find fault with others for the very things they themselves do and have done. This is why Jesus said, "Why do you see the speck in your neighbor's eye, but do not notice the log in your own eye? Or how can you say to your neighbor, 'Let me take the speck out of your eye,' while the log is in your own eye?" Friends, in humble obedience to our Lord Jesus Christ, let us first take the logs out of our own eyes in confession and repentance, and then, by God's grace, we may perhaps see clearly enough to assist our neighbors. Let us confess our sins.

PRAYER OF CONFESSION

Holy Lord, we confess we have been quick to judge others by standards we would never want applied to ourselves, and thus we have merited the same judgment. Surely the psalmist is right to lament, "There is no longer anyone who is godly; the faithful have disappeared from humankind." Forgive us, Lord, for our failures of faith, forgiveness, and gracious love. Forgive the duplicity of our hearts and the hypocrisy that arises between our words and our actions. Let our hearts be kindled anew by your gospel, the good news that you have done for us what we cannot do for ourselves, and thereby set us free and inspire us to fulfill the law and the prophets, acting graciously on behalf of others just as we have received grace upon grace from you, through Jesus Christ, your Son and our sovereign Savior.

DECLARATION OF FORGIVENESS

Hear the good news: Has anyone said to God, "I have endured punishment; I will not offend any more; teach me what I do not see; if I have done iniquity, I will do it no more"? To those who confess their sins and truly repent, the LORD says: "Because the poor are despoiled, because the needy groan, I will now rise up and place them in the safety for which they long." His divine power has thus given us everything needed for life and godliness, through the knowledge of him who called us by his own glory and goodness. Indeed, he has given us his precious and very great promises, so that through them we may escape from the corruption that is in the world because of lust, and may become participants of his divine nature. Therefore, friends, support your faith with goodness, knowledge, self-control, endurance, godliness, mutual affection, and love. Anyone who lacks these things is nearsighted and blind, forgetful of the cleansing of past sins, but if you practice them they will keep you from being ineffective and unfruitful in the knowledge of our Lord Jesus Christ. To you who have received the gift of saving faith through the righteousness of our God and Savior Jesus Christ: May grace and peace be yours in abundance in the knowledge of God and of Jesus our Lord, in whom we are well and truly forgiven.

Seventh Sunday after Epiphany / Proper 2
Ordinary Time 7

Job 35:1–16

Psalm 119: (1–16) 17–32

Matthew 7:13–20

2 Peter 2

Call to Worship

Because of their many troubles people cry out;
they call for help, for they are overwhelmed.

> Yet no one says, "Where is God my Maker,
> who gives strength in the night,
> who teaches us more than the animals of the earth,
> and makes us wiser than the birds of the air?"

Look at the heavens and see;
observe the clouds, which are higher than you.
If you sin, what do you accomplish against God?
And if your transgressions are multiplied, what do you do to him?

> What can the righteous give to God,
> or what does he receive from their hand?

Jesus said, "Enter through the narrow gate;
for the gate is wide and the road is easy that leads to destruction,
and there are many who take it.
But the gate is narrow and the road is hard that leads to life,
and there are few who find it."

> By all means, therefore, let us seek and enter the narrow gate,
> the way that leads to life. Let us worship God!

OPENING PRAYER

Come, O LORD, and revive us according to your word! Open our eyes, that we may behold your wondrous ways! Do not conceal yourself from your people, but strengthen us according to your promise. Put false ways far from us, and graciously teach us your way of truth and faithfulness. Enlarge our understanding and deal bountifully with your church, so that we may live according to your will. Make us remember and understand your ways, and we will meditate on your marvelous works, for the praise of your glory; this we ask in the name of Jesus Christ.

CALL TO CONFESSION

People are slaves to whatever masters them, and many who promise freedom and license in this world are themselves slaves of corruption. All too often, those who escape the defilements of the world through the knowledge of our Lord and Savior Jesus Christ are again entangled in them and overpowered, and their last state is worse than the first. God has not called us to degeneration, but to the righteousness of a regenerate life. Let us therefore confess our sins, and our need for true liberation from the powers of sin and death, to the only one who is able to deliver us, the one who alone has defeated sin and death by his death on the cross and by the power of his resurrection.

PRAYER OF CONFESSION

Spirit of the Living God, you have created us to know truth from falsehood and to bear good fruit that will last for eternity, yet we confess that we are often afraid to identify, expose, or admit what is false in our lives and to denounce lies when they threaten to lead your people astray, even unto death and destruction. Merciful Father, forgive our sin, our willful blindness, and the timidity that inhibits our testimony to the truth. Give us discernment, courage, and inspiration to be fully aware of your presence with us, your will for us. Give us fortitude, resolution, and true freedom, that we may be ever empowered to seek and hold fast to the straight and narrow way to life, for we know that you, our Lord Christ Jesus, are the way! This we ask in your holy name.

DECLARATION OF FORGIVENESS

Yes, people are slaves to whatever masters them, but those who repent and confess their sins in true humility have a good LORD who is unsurpassed, the Master who has bought them for freedom by the gift of his own Son. And if this same God, who saved Noah, a herald of righteousness, with seven others when he brought a flood on the world of the ungodly; if he rescued Lot, a righteous man greatly distressed by the licentiousness of the lawless, then the LORD knows how to rescue the godly from trial. For indeed the one who calls us to enter life through the narrow gate has struggled through that gate ahead of us, has opened the way for us, and thus has delivered us from death to life. Know that, in Jesus Christ, we are given the victory over sin that he himself gained on our behalf. Therefore, be at peace in the knowledge that in Christ we are forgiven and free to enter into the fullness of life.

Eighth Sunday after Epiphany / Proper 3
Ordinary Time 8

Job 36:1–23

Psalm 61

Matthew 13:53–58

2 Peter 3:1–7, 15–18

CALL TO WORSHIP

Surely God is mighty in strength of understanding.
Surely God does not despise any who are his.
> **In his justice he gives the afflicted their right.**
> **His eye is ever on the righteous.**
He sets kings on their thrones and they are exalted.
If they are bound and caught in affliction,
he declares to them their arrogant transgressions.
> **He opens their ears to instruction,**
> **and commands they return from iniquity.**
If they listen, and serve him, they prosper,
and spend their years in pleasantness.
If they do not listen, they perish and die without knowledge.
> **Let us therefore seek the LORD.**
> **Let us hear and heed his holy Word!**

OPENING PRAYER

Holy God, you are exalted in your power! By your word the heavens existed long ago and the whole earth was formed amidst the waters. Who is like you, our Creator and our only wise teacher? Who can prescribe your way for you or find any fault in you? Hear our pleas, O LORD, for we grow weary with the ways of this world. Lead us into your holy presence. Be our refuge and sanctuary from every enemy and from all who are false. Let your people take shelter under your loving arms and abide with you forever. For you, O God, hear our vows, and you grant a goodly heritage to those who fear your name. Therefore, we will ever sing praises to your name and walk humbly with you day after day, in the name of Christ Jesus our Lord.

CALL TO CONFESSION

Scripture warns us: Beware! Do not turn to iniquity. Because of sin, people are tried by affliction; the godless cherish anger and are enticed into scoffing. But God delivers the afflicted by their affliction, for he opens their ear by adversity. Indeed, he also patiently lifts them out of their distress, through repentance, into a broad place where there is no constraint. Let us, therefore, in penitence and faith, confess our sins to Almighty God.

PRAYER OF CONFESSION

Holy God, we confess that we stumble and fall short in matters of faith and obedience. We presume to be so familiar with you, or so knowledgable with regard to your will, that we impose limits on what you are able to do among us because of our unbelief. Not that we are able to so limit you, but in your grace you respect our decisions and allow us to live according to their results, to see how fruitless they are, and then you speak to us anew in order to arouse our sincere intention by reminding us of all that your prophets have said, and all that our Lord and Savior has spoken through your apostles. Forgive us, O Lord, for every sin, every rebellious and faithless act, every time we have refused to hear you. Forgive us for every time we have participated in the scoffing and the lust of this present age, or twisted the meaning of your words to suit our own desires, even when they lead to destruction. Rescue us, we pray, from the coming judgment, and in your merciful patience, restore to us the joy of your salvation. This we ask in the name of our living Savior and Lord Jesus Christ.

DECLARATION OF FORGIVENESS

Hear the good news! The Lord is not slow about his promise, but is patient, not wanting any to perish, but all to come to repentance. Therefore, beloved, as you wait for his appearing, strive to be found by him at peace, without spot or blemish, and regard his patience with you as your salvation. And do not turn the greatness of Christ's ransom or his wisdom into an occasion for stumbling, as though sin should abound in the greater space of his grace. For this is the error of the lawless and the unstable. Rather, use the freedom given you in faith and forgiveness in order to grow in the grace and knowledge of our Lord and Savior Jesus Christ, in whom we are truly redeemed, delivered, and saved. To him be the glory both now and to the day of eternity.

Last Sunday after Epiphany
(*Transfiguration Sunday*)

Job 36:24—37:24

Psalm 11

Matthew 8:5–13 OR John 4:43–54

Jude (OR Hebrews 13:9–14, 17–25, if Transfiguration preempts Ordinary Time 5)

CALL TO WORSHIP

The LORD is in his holy temple; the LORD's throne is in heaven.
His eyes behold, his gaze examines humankind.
> **For the LORD is righteous; he loves righteous deeds;**
> **the upright shall behold his face.**

Listen, listen to the thunder of his voice
and the rumbling that comes from his mouth.
> **God thunders wondrously with his voice;**
> **he does great things that we cannot comprehend.**

Surely God is great, and we do not know him;
the number of his years is unsearchable.
> **Remember to extol his work,**
> **of which mortals have sung.**

Can anyone understand the spreading of the clouds,
the thundering of his pavilion?
> **At this also my heart trembles, and leaps out of its place.**
> **Therefore mortals fear him; he does not regard any**
> **who are wise in their own conceit.**
> **Let us worship God.**

Opening Prayer

Almighty God, surrounded with golden splendor, you are awesome in your majesty! Who can look upon you in your radiance? You load the clouds with moisture and from your chamber comes the whirlwind and the rain. They turn round and round by your guidance, and accomplish on the earth all that you command. You say, "Fall on the earth," and the showers serve as a sign to everyone, so that all whom you have made may know you are God. Whether for correction, or for your creation, or for love, you cause it to happen, thus providing for people everywhere and giving food from heaven in abundance. Therefore, we praise you, O God. We give you thanks, O Lord, even as we seek sanctuary in you, our refuge, even as we take shelter in your holy loving presence, in the name of Jesus Christ, the Beloved of God.

Call to Confession

Stop and consider the wondrous works of God. Do you know how God lays his command upon them, and causes the lightning of his cloud to shine? Do you know the balancing of the clouds, the wondrous works of the one whose knowledge is perfect? Can you, like him, spread out the skies, hard as a molten mirror? What shall we say to him? Who can make a case before him amidst the darkness of this world? For he covers his hands with lightning and commands it to strike the mark. Its crashing tells about him; he is jealous with anger against iniquity. See, the Lord is coming with his holy ones, to execute judgment and convict everyone of all the deeds of ungodliness that they have committed and of all the harsh things that sinners have spoken against him. Nevertheless, our holy God is also merciful; he is able to keep you from falling and to make you stand without blemish in the presence of his glory with rejoicing. He is great in power and justice, and he will not violate righteousness when his people turn to him in repentance. Therefore, let us confess our sin to God.

Prayer of Confession

O Lord our God, who once for all saved a people out of the land of Egypt, yet allowed those who did not trust you to die in the wilderness, we confess that we, your people, have participated in the ungodliness of this age, turning your grace into license, indulging in immorality, and defiling the flesh. Forgive us, O Lord, for all our sins, for every foolish

and fruitless deed. Forgive us for each time we have refused your authority, spoken careless words without fear, or forgotten the greatness of your salvation and the faith that we share, the gospel with which we have been entrusted. Say the word, O Lord, and heal your servants. Be merciful, O God. Cleanse us and restore us to new life, equipping us with the mind of Christ Jesus, your beloved Son, in whose name we pray.

Declaration of Forgiveness

Remember the faithful witness to the authority of Jesus Christ who said, "Lord, I am not worthy to have you come under my roof; but only speak the word, and my servant will be healed." For Christ commended such faith, and he granted healing accordingly. Therefore, beloved, build yourselves up on your most holy faith, pray in the Holy Spirit, keep yourselves in the love of God, and receive the mercy of our Lord Jesus Christ that leads to eternal life. For in Jesus Christ we are forgiven, healed, and restored. Thanks be to God!

Benediction or Ascription of Praise [Jude 24–25]

Now to him who is able to keep you from falling, and to make you stand without blemish in the presence of his glory with rejoicing, to the only God our Savior, through Jesus Christ our Lord, be glory, majesty, power, and authority, before all time and now and forever. Amen.

OR

Benediction [Hebrews 13:20–21]

Now may the God of peace, who brought back from the dead our Lord Jesus, the great shepherd of the sheep, by the blood of the eternal covenant, make you complete in everything good so that you may do his will, working among us that which is pleasing in his sight, through Jesus Christ, to whom be the glory forever and ever. Amen.

PART II

The Paschal Cycle
Lent—Easter—Pentecost

Ash Wednesday

Isaiah 57:14–21

Psalm 102

John 5:1–18

James 1:1–16 OR Ephesians 2:11–22 OR Galatians 1:1–24

CALL TO WORSHIP [see Isaiah 57:14–21]

Build up, build up, prepare the way,
remove every obstruction from my people's way.
> For thus says the high and lofty one
> who inhabits eternity, whose name is Holy:
I dwell in the high and holy place,
and also with those who are contrite and humble in spirit,
> to revive the spirit of the humble,
> and to revive the heart of the contrite.
I will not continually accuse,
nor will I always be angry;
> for then their spirits would grow faint before me,
> even the souls that I have made.
I have seen their ways, but I will heal them;
I will lead them and repay them with comfort,
> creating for their mourners the fruit of the lips.
Peace, peace, to the far and the near, says the LORD;
> and I will heal them.

OPENING PRAYER

O God our heavenly Father, who, according to your gracious will, sent
Jesus Christ to set us free from the present evil age: we come with a history

63

of double-mindedness, and a thirst for your wisdom to make us faithful and true; we come with a habit of making excuses, and an earnest desire to be healthful and joyful. Draw near to us, we pray, and speak once more the unique and life-giving gospel of Jesus Christ, who gave himself for our sins and was raised from the dead, that we may be restored in spirit, soul, and body, and that your church might be reformed in accordance with your desire for us to be a holy nation. For you know, O Lord, that we are mortal, and in the midst of a busy life, we wither and fade as the flowers of the field. Renew us, therefore, before this earthly life is gone, that we may boast of your grace in raising us up from our lowly estate and giving us each a share in our Lord and Savior Jesus Christ, in whose name we pray.

Call to Confession

God has said, "There is no peace for the wicked. But they are like the tossing sea that cannot keep still; its waters toss up mire and mud." Do not be deceived, beloved. For one is tempted by one's own desire, being lured and enticed by it; then, when that desire has conceived, it gives birth to sin, and that sin, when it is fully grown, gives birth to death. No one, when tempted, should say, "I am being tempted by God"; for God cannot be tempted by evil, and he himself tempts no one. But blessed is anyone who overcomes temptation. Such a one has stood the test and will receive the crown of life that the Lord has promised to those who love him. Friends, in humility, let us confess to God the distress that sin has caused us and our need for the Lord's gracious redemption, that we may persevere in faith and obtain the crown of life.

Prayer of Confession [Psalm 102]

Hear my prayer, O Lord;
let my cry come to you.
> Do not hide your face from me
> in the day of my distress.
Incline your ear to me;
answer me speedily in the day when I call.
> For my days pass away like smoke,
> and my bones burn like a furnace.
My heart is stricken and withered like grass;
I am too wasted to eat my bread.

Because of my loud groaning
my bones cling to my skin.
I am like an owl of the wilderness,
like a little owl of the waste places.
I lie awake; I am like a lonely bird on the housetop.
All day long my enemies taunt me;
those who deride me use my name for a curse.
For I eat ashes like bread,
and mingle tears with my drink,
because of your indignation and anger;
for you have lifted me up and thrown me aside.
My days are like an evening shadow;
I wither away like grass.
But you, O Lord, are enthroned forever;
your name endures to all generations.
You will rise up and have compassion on Zion,
for it is time to favor it; the appointed time has come.
For your servants hold its stones dear,
and have pity on its dust.
The nations will fear the name of the Lord,
and all the kings of the earth your glory.
For the Lord will build up Zion;
he will appear in his glory.
He will regard the prayer of the destitute,
and will not despise their prayer.
Let this be recorded for a generation to come,
so that a people yet unborn may praise the Lord:
that he looked down from his holy height,
from heaven the Lord looked at the earth,
to hear the groans of the prisoners,
to set free those who were doomed to die;
so that the name of the Lord may be declared in Zion,
and his praise in Jerusalem,
when peoples gather together,
and kingdoms, to worship the Lord.
He has broken my strength in midcourse;
he has shortened my days.
"O my God," I say, "do not take me away

at the mid-point of my life,
> **you whose years endure**
> **throughout all generations."**
Long ago you laid the foundation of the earth,
and the heavens are the work of your hands.
> **They will perish, but you endure;**
> **they will all wear out like a garment.**
You change them like clothing, and they pass away;
but you are the same, and your years have no end.
> **The children of your servants shall live secure;**
> **their offspring shall be established in your presence.**

DECLARATION OF FORGIVENESS [Ephesians 2:12–22]

Remember that you were formerly without Christ, being aliens from the commonwealth of Israel, and strangers to the covenants of promise, having no hope and without God in the world. But now in Christ Jesus you who once were far off have been brought near by the blood of Christ. For Christ is our peace; in his flesh he has made both groups, Jew and Gentile, into one and has broken down the dividing wall, that is, the hostility between us. He has abolished the law with its commandment and ordinances, that he might create in himself one new humanity in place of the two, thus making peace, and might reconcile both groups to God in one body through the cross. So he came and proclaimed peace to you who were far off and peace to those who were near; for through him both have access in one Spirit to the Father. So then you are no longer strangers and aliens, but you are citizens with the saints and also members of the household of God, built upon the foundation of the apostles and prophets, with Christ Jesus himself as the cornerstone. In him the whole structure is joined together and grows into a holy temple in the Lord, in whom you also are built together spiritually into a dwelling place for God.

First Sunday in Lent

Deuteronomy 10:12–22 OR Nehemiah 9:1–38

Psalm 6

John 7:1–13

Galatians 2:1–14 (15–21) OR Galatians 1:1–24 OR James 1:1–27 OR James 1:17—2:13

CALL TO WORSHIP

You shall fear the LORD your God; him alone you shall worship.
To the LORD you shall hold fast, and by his name you shall swear.
    The LORD is our praise; he is our God, who has done
    great and awesome things for us that our own eyes have seen.
Heaven and the heaven of heavens belong to the LORD our God,
the earth with all that is in it!
    The LORD, the great God, is God of gods and LORD of lords.
    Mighty and awesome, he is not partial and he takes no bribe.
Circumcise your heart, and do not be stubborn any longer,
for what does the LORD your God require of you?
    Only to fear the LORD, to walk in all his ways, to love him,
    to serve him with all our heart and soul, and to keep
    his commandments and decrees for our own well-being.

OPENING PRAYER

O LORD our God, draw near to us and receive our thanksgiving and praise, for you have given us a gospel that is not of human origin, but one that originated with you and that you revealed through and in your Son, our Savior, the Lord Jesus Christ. Come, O Lord, in the power of your Spirit, and let your presence, your voice, your Word be revealed to those whom you have summoned here this day, you who have graciously set your heart in love upon your people Israel, through whom salvation has come into the world, you who, still more graciously, have extended your grace and freedom to us through your self-sacrificing Son. Now, in this hour, let there be no doubt among us that you yourself are here, and let there be seen from the heights of ecclesial and worldly power that a flame is kindled here, a signal fire of faith and truth and holiness and grace, of joy and freedom and unity and patience, of hope and blessedness and strength and peace. Come, O Lord, in the person of your Spirit.

CALL TO CONFESSION

Let us not worry about human approval, but let us seek God's approval above all. Let us no longer live so as to please people, but rather, let us aim to be servants of Christ. We live in a world so loved by God that God sent his only Son to save it. Yet, this same world in which we live, this world so loved by God, hates the Lord Jesus, because according to his own testimony, Jesus testifies against it that its works are evil. Though we are called to keep ourselves unstained by this world, none of us has been able to do so. Therefore, let us confess and renounce and repent fully of the sin that puts enmity between us and God and that destroys our relations with one another.

PRAYER OF CONFESSION

O LORD, what evil and wickedness, what confusion and sickness we see in the world! Everywhere truth is perverted, and those whom you have called in the grace of Christ are deserting you and turning to a different gospel—not that there is another gospel! Forgive us, Lord Jesus, and forgive your church for the ways in which we ourselves have become confused or have contributed to the confusion! Forgive us, O Father, for each way in which we ourselves have perverted the gospel of Christ, or have allowed others to pervert it, whether by wrong action or inaction, whether by false speech or a failure to speak on behalf of your Son. Forgive us, O Spirit, wherever we have, by thought, word, or deed, intentionally or unintentionally, persecuted Christ's body, the church, and distorted your message of penitence and faith, salvation and grace, freedom and love! Be gracious, O LORD, for we are languishing! Turn,

O Holy LORD, save your church and deliver us for the sake of your steadfast love, in Christ Jesus our Lord!

DECLARATION OF FORGIVENESS

Hear again the good news, as though for the first time! The Lord Jesus Christ gave himself for our sins to set us free from the present evil age. The victory that he has won on your behalf is such that I may say, and you may believe, with the authority of him who has revealed the gospel and commissioned us to proclaim it: the LORD has heard your weeping and your supplication; the LORD accepts your prayer. Now let every enemy of the gospel, every enemy of the faithful, be struck with terror, let every tempter be ashamed, let every cause of stumbling be removed from before you, that you may walk, without stumbling, without wandering, without wavering, in the strength of the gospel of Jesus Christ.

Second Sunday in Lent

Ezekiel 47:1–12

Psalm 143

John 7:14–39

James 2: (14–17) 18–26 OR James 2:1–26 OR Galatians 2:1–14 (15–21)

CALL TO WORSHIP

Jesus said, "Let anyone who is thirsty come to me,
and let the one who believes in me drink."
    **Indeed, "out of the believer's heart shall flow
    rivers of living water."**
When the river that flows from the threshold of the temple
enters the sea of stagnant waters, the water will become fresh.
    Everything will live where the river goes.
    There will grow all kinds of trees yielding fruit.
Their leaves will not wither nor their fruit fail,
because the water for them flows from the sanctuary.
    Their fruit will be for food and their leaves for healing.
    Living God, let us hear of your steadfast love in the morning!

OPENING PRAYER

O LORD our God, you are the One true source of Living Water, the One
who has been revealed in Christ Jesus, crucified, risen, and glorified, the
One who sends the Spirit to summon your church into life anew! Give us
life, O God, for we thirst for you! Give us freedom, O Christ, for we are
bound to you! Give us courage, O Spirit, for we would have you lead us
into the waters that flow from life unto life, from deep unto deep, from the

heart of the very temple of God to the heart of those who believe in and love you. This we ask in your holy name.

CALL TO CONFESSION

Remember the days of old, and think about all the deeds of God! Meditate on the works of his hands, and stretch out your hands to him. For the one who is thirsty like a parched land will find relief in the living waters of Christ's mercy. To the one who is crushed under the weight of sin, to the one who sits in the darkness of the Pit, to the one whose spirit faints and fails, Christ is the way to freedom and forgiveness. Therefore, seek the Lord, seek his face, confess your sin and your faith in him, for he will answer you quickly and will not delay in forgiving the penitent heart.

PRAYER OF CONFESSION

Hear our prayer, O LORD, and give ear to our confession, O you who are always faithful! Do not enter into judgment with your servants, for no one living is righteous before you. We ourselves have not always walked in conformity to the truth of the gospel, nor have we consistently remembered the poor. Though we profess belief, we have produced scant evidence, far too few good works, to show that our faith is alive and well. Forgive us for our transgressions, O God, and for our unfaithfulness. Give us courage, even now, to be crucified with Christ, to die to the law that condemns us, that we might ever live to you, through faith in your Son, and that he might, now and forever, live in each of our hearts and enliven your church, for the glory of your name.

DECLARATION OF FORGIVENESS

You who have fled to the LORD for refuge, now live by faith in the Son of God, who has given himself for you in love. Discipline yourselves under the teaching of him whose good Spirit leads you on a level path. For the freedom we have in Christ Jesus is freedom to walk on the side of truth and to conform our lives faithfully to the One who has justified us by his faith.

Third Sunday in Lent

Genesis 13 OR 2 Samuel 7:18–29

Psalm 38

John 7:40–52

Galatians 3:1–22 OR James 3:1–18

CALL TO WORSHIP

The LORD has promised, saying, "Raise your eyes now,
and look to the north, the south, the east, and the west . . ."
> **You are great, O LORD our God; for there is no one like you;**
> **there is no God besides you, according to all that we have heard!**
"For all the land that you see
I will give to you and to your offspring forever.
I will make your offspring like the dust of the earth."
> **Now, LORD God, as for the word that you have spoken,**
> **confirm it forever; do as you have promised!**
"If one can count the dust of the earth,
your offspring also can be counted.
Rise up, walk through the length and the breadth of the land,
for I will give it to you."
> **Thus your name will be magnified forever!**
> **For you are God, and your words are true!**

OPENING PRAYER

Because of your promise, O God, and according to your own heart, you have done great things and have revealed yourself to your servants, through your Son Jesus Christ, who is Abraham's seed and the Son of David! Who is like your people Israel, through whom Christ our salvation has come into the world? Is there another nation on earth whose God has redeemed them as a people, so as to make a name for himself, by driving out other nations and their gods? Yet you have established your people Israel as yours forever! You, O LORD, have become their God and ours! You, the Lord of hosts, are God over Israel, and the house of your servant David is established forever in your Son, the obedient one, Jesus Christ. For you, the God of Israel, once said to your servant David, "I will build you a house," and "Unless the LORD builds the house, those who build it labor in vain." Therefore, we have courage to pray this prayer to you. Because of your promise, O God, and according to your own heart, please bless this house so that it, too, though but a humble reflection of the house of David, may continue forever in the name and in the Spirit of Christ; for you, O Lord God, have spoken, and with your blessing we, your people, shall be blessed forever, in Jesus' name.

CALL TO CONFESSION

The law has imprisoned all things under the power of sin, so that what was promised through faith in Jesus Christ might be given to those who believe. Yet, despite our best efforts to live in faith, all of us make many mistakes. Anyone who makes no mistakes in speaking is already perfect. Yet who can tame the tongue—a restless evil, full of deadly poison? With it we bless the Lord and Father, and with it we curse those who are made in the image of God. From the same mouth come blessing and curse, but this should not be so. If we have bitter envy and selfish ambition in our hearts, there will be also disorder and wickedness of every kind. Yet confession itself is an act of faith when it proceeds from a heart that longs to be free of such things.

PRAYER OF CONFESSION [Adapted from Psalm 38]

O LORD, do not issue your rebuke in anger or administer discipline in your wrath. For our iniquities have overwhelmed us, and they weigh like a burden too heavy to bear. We are spent; we are crushed. Our hearts throb and our strength fails at the remembrance of sins we cannot undo. Yet you know the longing of each heart, the depth of our groaning, and our sighing is not hidden from you. It is for you, O God, that we wait, and it is you who will answer. We confess our iniquity; we are sorry for our sin. Only do not let your enemies rejoice over us.

Redeem and forgive us, O LORD. Do not forsake your people, and do not be far from us; but make haste to help us, O LORD, our salvation! We ask this in Jesus' name.

DECLARATION OF FORGIVENESS

Christ has redeemed us from the curse of the law by becoming a curse for us, for it is written, "Cursed is everyone who hangs on a tree." Thus, the blessing of Abraham has come to the Gentiles, and so to us, that we too might receive the promise of the Spirit through faith in Christ Jesus! Before faith came, we were imprisoned and guarded under the law until faith was revealed. But now that faith has come, in Christ Jesus, you are children of God through faith. As many of you as were baptized into Christ have clothed yourselves with Christ. If you belong to Christ, then you are Abraham's seed, heirs according to the promise. In your freedom as children, in the freedom of faith, receive the wisdom from above that is first pure, then peaceable, gentle, willing to yield, full of mercy and good fruits, without a trace of partiality or hypocrisy. For a harvest of righteousness is sown in peace for those who make peace. Be at peace and bear good fruit as you live in Christ, for Christ himself has made peace with God on our behalf.

Fourth Sunday in Lent

Isaiah 54:1–4 (5–14) 15–17 OR Isaiah 37:14–38

Psalm 39

John 8:12–30

James 4:4–17 OR Galatians 4:1—5:1

CALL TO WORSHIP

Sing, O barren one who did not bear!
Burst into song and shout, you who have not been in labor!
For the children of the desolate woman will be more
than the children of her that is married, says the LORD.
Enlarge the site of your tent; let the curtains be stretched out;
do not hold back; lengthen your cords, and strengthen your stakes.
For you will spread out to the right and to the left,
and your descendants will possess the nations, says the LORD.
Do not fear, for you will not be ashamed;
do not be discouraged, for you will not suffer disgrace.
Let all of our children be taught by the LORD,
and then shall our children prosper.

OPENING PRAYER

Our Lord Jesus Christ, light for the world, you who are from above and
not of this world, you are truly the Son of God, the Son of Man, the Savior
of all who trust in you. For you have been lifted up, crucified, for the sins
of the world. Allow us now, we humbly pray, to lift you up in exaltation,
thanksgiving, and praise, that you might draw all to yourself, and speak
your Word of life and of truth, as the Father has instructed. Let us receive
your Spirit into our hearts, that as you call out to our heavenly Father, we

75

might be awakened to your presence within us, always working to bring us safely home.

CALL TO CONFESSION

Friendship with the world is enmity with God. Therefore, whoever wishes to be a friend of the world becomes an enemy of God. God yearns jealously for the spirit that he has made to dwell in us. But he gives all the more grace; thus, the Spirit says, "God opposes the proud, but gives grace to the humble." Therefore, let us resist the enemy that he might flee from us, and let us be humble and submit ourselves to God, for when we draw near to the Lord, the Lord draws near to us.

PRAYER OF CONFESSION

O Lord, we confess that our hands are unclean and our hearts impure with our double-minded efforts to serve two masters, both you and the world. Forgive us, O God, and deliver us from all our transgressions, for all our hope is in you. Help us know our end and the measure of our days; remind us how fleeting is life, far too short to be wasted in folly, but a mere breath, a mere shadow. Do not be silent at our sorrow, or unmoved by our tears for what we cannot undo. Remove our sins from us, O God, and set us free by the Spirit of grace, that we may live forever as your joyful and grateful children, through Christ Jesus, in whose name we pray.

DECLARATION OF FORGIVENESS

The LORD has said, "This is like the days of Noah to me: Just as I swore that the waters of Noah would never again go over the earth, so I have sworn that I will not be angry with you and will not rebuke you. For the mountains may depart and the hills be removed, but my steadfast love shall not depart from you, and my covenant of peace shall not be removed, says the LORD, who has compassion on you. . . . If anyone stirs up strife, it is not from me; whoever stirs up strife with you shall fall because of you. . . . This is the heritage of the servants of the LORD and their vindication from me, says the LORD. No weapon that is fashioned against you shall prosper, and you shall confute every tongue that rises against you in judgment." Friends, know, believe, and receive this good news: by the grace of our Lord Jesus Christ, we are forgiven and made free.

Fifth Sunday in Lent

Genesis 4:1–16 OR Isaiah 63: (7–9) 10–19

Psalm 101

John 8:31–47

Galatians 5: (1) 2–12 (13–25) 26 OR James 5:1–20

CALL TO WORSHIP

The LORD has said, "Surely my children will not deal falsely,"
and he has become their savior.
> **In all their distress he was distressed,**
> **and the angel of his presence saved them.**
In his love and in his pity he redeemed them;
he lifted them up and carried them all the days of old.
> **Look down from heaven, O LORD, and regard us now**
> **from your holy and glorious habitation!**
Where are your zeal, your might, and the yearning of your heart?
Do not withhold your compassion from your people!
> **For you are our Father, though Israel does not acknowledge us;**
> **you, O LORD, are our Father;**
> **our Redeemer from of old is your name.**

OPENING PRAYER

O Lord, compassionate and merciful, you have called us to freedom, to live and be guided by your Spirit, to bear the fruit of the Spirit, to serve one another in love and to love one another as we love ourselves! Let us not continue to live as those who have failed to come under the rule of your Son, or as those who are not called by the name of your Christ. But refresh us with your presence and anoint us with your Spirit, that our praises might be pleasing to you and our prayers might be powerful and effective on behalf of those who have become weak in the faith or have wandered from you. You, who stand at the very doors of this place, enter and speak once again to your people! Give us strength for the life of faith, endurance as we eagerly await your final coming, and patience as we long for, and summon others into, your holy and gracious presence. This we ask in Jesus' name.

CALL TO CONFESSION

The Lord is gracious toward his children. But when we rebel, we grieve the Holy Spirit, we become enemies of God through sin, and God himself opposes us. At such times, sin lurks at the door, desiring to corrupt and lead us away from God, but we must master it. Jesus said, "Very truly, I tell you, everyone who commits sin is a slave to sin. The slave does not have a permanent place in the household; but the Son has a place forever. So if the Son makes you free, you will be free indeed." Thus, God's will for us is that we should no longer be slaves to sin, but that we should take authority over sin and subdue it, thus assuming our place in freedom as children of God in Christ and through Christ. Therefore, let us confess our sins to God and in the presence of one another, that we may be healed and restored. For the prayer of faith will save the sick—the Lord himself will raise them up—and anyone who has committed sins will be forgiven.

PRAYER OF CONFESSION

God of truth, you have said that the one who practices deceit shall not remain in your house, and the one who utters lies shall not continue in your presence. Therefore, we offer you our honest confession. For we have neither studied nor attained the way that is blameless. We have seen evil and set base things before our eyes. We have allowed the desires of our hearts to be perverted and our integrity to be corrupted. Forgive us, O LORD, for falling behind—and sometimes even falling away! Forgive us for misusing our freedom, for seeking and seizing opportunities for self-indulgence. But, as we reach up to you now in humility, help us walk in faith, that you might look with favor on the faithful in the land, that we might live with you forever, serve you blamelessly, and sing of loyalty and of justice; yes, to you, O LORD, we will sing!

Declaration of Forgiveness

Whoever is from God hears the words of God, for through the Spirit, by faith, we now have the hope of righteousness. In freedom, let us live by the Spirit, no longer gratifying the desires of the flesh, but freely obeying the truth! For though the world takes offense at the cross of Jesus Christ, we know that Christ Jesus is the truth, and in him the only thing that counts is faith working through love. As Jesus said: "If you continue in my word, you are truly my disciples; and you will know the truth, and the truth will make you free." Therefore, be free, for those who belong to Christ Jesus have crucified the flesh with its passions and desires, and every sin that once kept you in darkness and slavery has been forgiven.

Sixth Sunday in Lent (*Palm Sunday*)

Deuteronomy 11:1–17 OR Isaiah 43:8–15

Psalm 94 OR 35

John 8:48–59

Romans 1:8–15 (16–17) 18–32; 2:1–11 OR Galatians 6:1–18

CALL TO WORSHIP

"You are my witnesses," says the LORD,
"and my servant whom I have chosen."
> **O LORD, who is like you? You deliver the weak from those**
> **too strong for them, the needy from those who despoil them.**
"Know and believe and understand that I am he.
Before me no god was formed, nor shall there be any after me."
> **The LORD is God! Who can deliver from his hand?**
> **When he works, who can hinder it?**
The LORD says, "I, I am the LORD, and beside me there is no savior.
I declared and saved and proclaimed, and you are my witnesses."
> **Let us love the LORD our God, and serve only him,**
> **for the LORD is our help, whose steadfast love bears us up.**

OPENING PRAYER

Our Lord Jesus Christ, you who came not seeking your own glory but that of our heavenly Father, you have promised that those who keep your word will never see death. Therefore, come and speak once again to the glory of the Father, that we might receive your word anew and hold fast to it. As you appeared before Abraham, who rejoiced and was glad that he saw your day, so make your presence known among us now, that the glory which the Father seeks on your behalf and the great deeds that you would do in our midst might be seen by our own eyes and by those of this generation. For it is we ourselves who must acknowledge the greatness of the Lord, the signs and the deeds that you, the Father, the Son, and the Holy Spirit, have done and are doing with your mighty hand and your outstretched arm. Come, Lord! For we are your witnesses and you are our salvation!

CALL TO CONFESSION

God is neither mocked nor deceived, for we reap whatever we sow. If we sow to the flesh, we will reap corruption from the flesh; but if we sow to the Spirit, we will reap eternal life from the Spirit. Take care, for the anger of the Lord is kindled when we allow ourselves to be seduced into turning away from him to worship and serve other gods. But, when we know nothing except the cross of our Lord Jesus Christ, regarding the world as crucified to the self and the self as crucified to the world, then there is a new creation! Truly, God promises peace and mercy to those who confess their sins and place their trust in the crucified Savior.

PRAYER OF CONFESSION

O God our Creator, we confess that we are without excuse, for though we know you in part, we often fail to honor you as God or give you thanks. We have allowed futility, senselessness, and darkness to overtake our thoughts, which are but an empty breath. Claiming wisdom, we have acted foolishly, exchanging your glory for lifeless images and the truth about you for the lies of the world. We have worshiped your creatures and our own creations rather you, our Creator, who alone are holy and blessed forever! Forgive us, O God, for our impurity and for every lapse into idolatry! Protect us, O God, against every temptation and every tempter. Rise up and contend with those who contend with your people, that we, with your help, might learn how to desire and choose the right, the good, and the true. For without you, O Lord, we have no hope of peace or prosperity; apart from you, we can do nothing.

DECLARATION OF FORGIVENESS

Thus says the LORD, your Redeemer, the Holy One of Israel: "For your sake I will send to Babylon and break down all the bars, and the shouting of your captors will be turned to lamentation. I am the LORD, the Holy

One, the Creator of Israel, your King." Those who learn and practice the discipline of the LORD are blessed, and happy are those whom the word of the LORD instructs. For the LORD does not forsake his people or abandon his heritage; but justice will return to the righteous, and all the upright in heart will follow it. God's kindness is meant to lead you to repentance, and the gospel of Jesus Christ is the power of God for salvation to everyone who has faith. For in the gospel the righteousness of God is revealed through faith for faith. Therefore, live by faith, as is befitting the upright people of God. Know that you are forgiven, and be at peace.

Maundy Thursday

Deuteronomy 30:1–14

Psalm 113

John 7:53–8:11 OR Luke 22:1–38 (39–46)

Romans 2:12–29

CALL TO WORSHIP

Love the LORD your God with all your heart
and with all your soul, in order that you may live.
> **Let the greatest become like the youngest,**
> **and the leader like one who serves.**

This commandment is not too hard for you, nor is it too far away.
No, the word is very near to you; it is in your mouth and in your heart.
> **For who is greater, the one at the table or the one who serves?**
> **But our Lord is among us as one who serves!**

Who is like the LORD our God, who is seated on high?
Yet he raises the poor from the dust, and lifts the needy from the ashes.
> **O LORD, raise us up and out of our need, that by your grace**
> **we might eat and drink at your table in your kingdom.**

OPENING PRAYER

May your name blessed, O LORD our God, from this time on and forever-more. May your name be praised, O King of the universe, from the rising of the sun to its setting. For you, O LORD, are high above the nations, and your glory reaches far above the heavens. Yet the lonely and despised are not beyond your care, but you exalt the lowly and discern the thoughts of those who are far away. You search out the human heart, giving joy and blessing to those who love you, convicting the conscience of the one who has turned away. Now, as we consider all that Christ Jesus your Son endured for our salvation, let your Spirit draw us together in remembrance of his ministry, his words, his obedience, his suffering, his serving, and his grace. For such is your goodness as we have seen it in Jesus, who took upon himself the condemnation and the death that we ourselves have deserved.

CALL TO CONFESSION

Return to the LORD your God; obey him with all your heart and soul. Then the LORD will restore your fortunes, show you his compassion, and gather you to himself. But do not ignore the voice of the conscience as it bears witness to the truth, nor resolve your conflicting thoughts apart from the Lord Jesus Christ, who will one day judge the secret thoughts of all. Rather, let us submit them all to our Savior and Judge, that we may settle our account for the sake of a clear conscience, and pray that we may not come to the time of trial.

PRAYER OF CONFESSION

Almighty God, whose finger engraved the tablets of the law, whose word exposes the intentions of the heart, we confess that we are in need of all the grace that your Son has shown by standing between our accusers and us, and by taking upon himself the punishment for sin. Where the enemy would sift your people like wheat, we ask that our sins would be thoroughly forgiven, and that your Son, our intercessor, would pray that our faith might never fail. Keep us, O God, from times of trial and testing. Give us strength in the joy that was set before your Son, the joy of the Lord, for which Christ Jesus endured the cross, that we might in turn encourage one another to place our faith and our hope in him.

DECLARATION OF FORGIVENESS

Truly with Christ, we lack no good thing. For he himself is our defender, our mediator, who intercedes for us where the law would condemn us. For when Jesus, the living Word of God, says, "Let the one who is without sin cast the first stone," there is soon no one left to condemn the sinner, none but him who also says, "Neither do I condemn you. Go your way, and from now on do not sin again." This is the gracious and loving nature of our Servant Lord, who alone has fully kept the law, and who, at the same time, has taken its condemnation upon himself. For our loving Lord, rather than condemning, delights in prospering you, and this he will do, as you learn to be like him, following him in obedience and faith. Truly it is for the sake of forgiveness and salvation that Christ Jesus the Truth has come into the world. Therefore, know that you are forgiven, and be at peace.

Good Friday

Ezra 9:5–15 OR Jeremiah 25:15–38 OR 2 Chronicles 7:1–22

Psalm 88

Luke 23: (1–12) 13–49

1 Peter 4:1–19

CALL TO WORSHIP [see Jeremiah 25]

Thus says the LORD of hosts:
See, I am summoning a sword
against all the inhabitants of the earth.
> **The LORD will roar from on high,**
> **and from his holy habitation utter his voice;**
> **he will roar mightily against his fold,**
> **and shout, like those who tread the grapes,**
> **against all the inhabitants of the earth.**
The clamor will resound to the ends of the earth,
for the LORD has an indictment against the nations;
he is entering into judgment with all flesh,
and the guilty he will put to the sword, says the LORD.
> **Thus says the LORD of hosts:**
> **See, disaster is spreading from nation to nation,**
> **and a great tempest is stirring**
> **from the farthest parts of the earth!**
Wail, you shepherds, and cry out;
roll in ashes, you lords of the flock,
for you shall fall like a choice vessel
and there shall be no escape for the LORDS of the flock.
> **Hark! the cry of the shepherds,**

and the wailing of the lords of the flock!
For the LORD is despoiling their pasture,
and the peaceful folds are devastated,
because of the fierce anger of the LORD.
> **Like a lion he has left his covert;**
> **for their land has become a waste**
> **because of the cruel sword and his fierce anger.**
Come, let us bow down and surrender
to the holy and righteous One:
> **God the LORD, the Holy Spirit,**
> **and Jesus Christ the Son of God.**

RESPONSIVE PSALM [Psalm 88]

O LORD, God of my salvation,
when at night I cry out in your presence,
let my prayer come before you;
incline your ear to my cry.
> **For my soul is full of troubles,**
> **and my life draws near to Sheol.**
I am counted among those who go down to the Pit;
I am like those who have no help,
like those forsaken among the dead,
like the slain that lie in the grave,
like those whom you remember no more,
for they are cut off from your hand.
> **You have put me in the depths of the Pit,**
> **in the regions dark and deep.**
Your wrath lies heavy upon me,
and you overwhelm me with all your waves.
> **You have caused my companions to shun me;**
> **you have made me a thing of horror to them.**
I am shut in so that I cannot escape;
my eye grows dim through sorrow.
> **Every day I call on you, O LORD;**
> **I spread out my hands to you.**
> **Do you work wonders for the dead?**
> **Do the shades rise up to praise you?**

Is your steadfast love declared in the grave,
or your faithfulness in Abaddon?
Are your wonders known in the darkness,
or your saving help in the land of forgetfulness?

> **But I, O LORD, cry out to you;**
> **in the morning my prayer comes before you.**
> **O LORD, why do you cast me off?**
> **Why do you hide your face from me?**

Wretched and close to death from my youth up,
I suffer your terrors; I am desperate.
Your wrath has swept over me;
your dread assaults destroy me.

> **They surround me like a flood all day long;**
> **from all sides they close in on me.**
> **You have caused friend and neighbor to shun me;**
> **my companions are in darkness.**

CALL TO CONFESSION

The time has come for judgment to begin with the household of God. Surely we have already spent enough time in doing what unbelievers do, living in licentiousness, passions, drunkenness, reveling, carousing, and lawless idolatry. All who do such things must give an accounting to him who stands ready to judge the living and the dead. Yet the LORD has also promised, as he did to Solomon, "if my people who are called by my name humble themselves, pray, seek my face, and turn from their wicked ways, then I will hear from heaven, and will forgive their sin and heal their land," and "my eyes will be open and my ears attentive to the prayer that is made in this place." How much more then will God, who alone is good, whose steadfast love endures forever, hear the prayers of the Son of God, who has interceded for sinners from the cross itself and now prays for us at the right hand of power? Therefore, let us entrust ourselves to our faithful Creator, approaching our God through Christ, with penitence, humility, and faith, and confessing our sin to our righteous and merciful Redeemer.

PRAYER OF CONFESSION [Adapted from Ezra 9]

O LORD our God, how can we lift our faces to you? For our iniquities have risen higher than our heads, and our guilt has mounted up to the heavens. From the days of our ancestors to the present, we have been deep in guilt, and we are ashamed of all our iniquities. For we have forsaken your commandments and filled the land from end to end with uncleanness. And now, our God, what shall we say? Here we are before you in our guilt, and no one can face you claiming to be righteous, no one but Jesus Christ, the Righteous One himself. After all that has come upon us for our sins and our great guilt, you, our God, have not punished us as our iniquities deserve; you have not forsaken us but have extended your steadfast love to us, to give us new life in Christ. Forgive us, therefore, O merciful God, for the sake of your gracious Son, Jesus Christ, that his great suffering and his redeeming work might bring us fully into eternal fellowship with you, and that we might commit and commend our spirits, as he has done, into your loving and gracious hand.

DECLARATION OF FORGIVENESS [see Luke 23 and 1 Peter 4]

Truly Jesus our Messiah came not to save himself but to save sinners. In his suffering on the cross, and in his prayer that even his executioners might be forgiven, he who was found guiltless has atoned for our guilt and secured the salvation of all those who, though formerly his enemies, now trust in him whose love covers a multitude of sins. For this is the reason the gospel was proclaimed even to you who were once dead in your sins—that you too might live in the Spirit as God does, no longer by human desires but by the will of God and with all the strength that God supplies, so that God may be glorified in all things through Jesus Christ, in whom we are forgiven and to whom, with the Father and the Spirit, belongs all glory and power, forever and ever. Blessed be God forever! Amen!

Holy Saturday: The Great Vigil

Numbers 10:33–36; Deuteronomy 10:11—12:1; Judges 5:1–31; Song 4:9—5:16; Isaiah 26:1–21

Psalms 7; 17; 44; 57 OR 108; 119:145–176; 149

Matthew 7:1–23; Luke 7:36—8:3; Matthew 27:62–66

1Corinthians 15: (20–26) 27–50 (51–58)

CALL TO WORSHIP [see Isaiah 26:4, 8–9, 12–14, 18a–19]

Trust in the LORD forever,
for in the LORD God you have an everlasting rock.
> In the path of your judgments, O LORD, we wait for you;
> your name and your renown are the soul's desire.
My soul yearns for you in the night,
my spirit within me earnestly seeks you.
> For when your judgments are in the earth,
> the inhabitants of the world learn righteousness.
O LORD, you will ordain peace for us,
for indeed, all that we have done, you have done for us.
> O LORD our God, other lords besides you have ruled over us,
> but we acknowledge your name alone.
The dead do not live; shades do not rise—
because you have punished and destroyed them,
and wiped out all memory of them.
> We have won no victories on earth,
> and no one is born to inhabit the world.
Your dead shall live, their corpses shall rise.
O dwellers in the dust, awake and sing for joy!
> For your dew is a radiant dew,
> and the earth will give birth to those long dead.

90

OPENING PRAYER

O LORD our God, you alone are our God; you alone are our praise, for you have done great and awesome things that our own eyes have seen. You alone are worthy of worship and to you alone shall we hold fast. Although heaven and the heaven of heavens belong to you, O LORD, with the earth and all that is in it, yet you graciously set your heart in love on our ancestors and chose us, their descendants, from among the nations, as it is today. Our ancestors went down to Egypt seventy persons and returned a mighty nation, saved from death by the sign of the blood of the Paschal Lamb, and preserved through the baptismal waters of the Red Sea. When your Son Jesus Christ came, he fulfilled the old covenant and became for us the Lamb who takes away the sin of the world, and offered us the living water of eternal life in the Spirit, and through this Christ you have made your people—both Jew and Gentile—into one body, one people, as numerous as the stars of heaven. Mindful of Christ's death for us, and revived by the good news of his resurrection, circumcise our hearts, O LORD, that no stubbornness would harden them, no deception make us stumble, and no worldliness blind us to your presence, your word, your will, or your Spirit. For you, O LORD our God—Father, Son, and Holy Spirit—are God of gods and Lord of lords, the great God, mighty and awesome, who, in Jesus Christ, have exercised sovereignty over death, vindicating his sinless life by crushing Satan under his feet. Come, O God, and make your presence known to us once again, as we offer prayers of praise and adoration, in the name of Jesus Christ.

CALL TO CONFESSION

Flesh and blood cannot inherit the kingdom of God, nor does the perishable inherit the imperishable. But the apostle speaks of dying daily in light of the powerful certainty of the resurrection of Jesus, by which we shall face every danger and boast of our hope in Christ Jesus our Lord. For if the dead are not raised, what good is our hope? But it is with no merely human hope that we believe in this gospel. Instead, with a sober and right mind, we have a hope that is built on the words of Christ himself and on the reality of his resurrection. Therefore, with confidence in the gracious mercy of God, we confess our sin, considering ourselves henceforth dead to its power, and we ask the Lord of the Resurrection to forgive our past sins and give us new life.

Responsive Prayer of Confession [Psalm 119:169–176]

Let my cry come before you, O Lord;
    give me understanding according to your word.
Let my supplication come before you;
    deliver me according to your promise.
My lips will pour forth praise,
    because you teach me your statutes.
My tongue will sing of your promise,
    for all your commandments are right.
Let your hand be ready to help me,
    for I have chosen your precepts.
I long for your salvation, O Lord,
    and your law is my delight.
Let me live that I may praise you,
    and let your ordinances help me.
I have gone astray like a lost sheep;
    seek out your servant,
    for I do not forget your commandments.

Declaration of Forgiveness

Not all flesh is alike: some have no knowledge of God, but we are called to sin no more, to love the Lord our God, and to serve him with all our heart and with all our soul. Just as we have borne the image of the man of dust, we will also bear the image of the man of heaven. As was the man of dust, so are those who are of the dust; and as is the man of heaven, so are those who are of heaven. The first Adam was from the earth, a man of dust; the second Adam is from heaven. But it is not the spiritual that is first, but the physical, and then the spiritual. Thus it is written, "The first Adam became a living being"; the last Adam, Jesus Christ, has become a life-giving spirit. So it is with the resurrection of the dead. What is sown is perishable, what is raised is imperishable. It is sown in dishonor, it is raised in glory. It is sown in weakness, it is raised in power. It is sown a physical body, it is raised a spiritual body. If there is a physical body, there is also a spiritual body. Know, therefore, that in our baptism into Christ, we share both his death and his resurrection. He who has taken on and redeemed human flesh from sin has forgiven our sins and given us his Spirit as living water, the water of eternal life itself. Thanks be to God the Father, God the Son, and God the Holy Spirit for our new, redeemed second nature, in Christ!

EXHORTATION [Deuteronomy 10:12–13]

So now, what does the LORD your God require of you? Only to fear the LORD your God, to walk in all his ways, to love him, to serve the LORD your God with all your heart and with all your soul, and to keep the commandments of the LORD your God for your own well-being.

Easter (*The Resurrection of the Lord*)

Deuteronomy 7:1–26

Psalm 75 OR 76

John 5:19–30

2 Corinthians 1:1–17 (18–22)

Just as the Father raises the dead and gives them life,
so the Son gives life to whomever he wishes.
> **Let all honor be given to the risen Son of God,**
> **to God the Father, and to God the Holy Spirit.**
Jesus says, "Very truly, I tell you, anyone who hears my word
and believes him who sent me has eternal life."
> **The hour is coming—and this is the hour!—**
> **when the dead will hear the voice of the Son of God.**
"Those who hear will live; whoever believes does not
come under judgment, but has passed from death to life."
> **Those in their graves will hear his voice and be raised—**
> **those who have done good, to the resurrection of life,**
> **and those who have done evil, to the resurrection of condemnation.**

OR

It was not because you were more numerous than any other people
that the LORD set his heart on you and chose you.
> **How can we claim to be any greater**
> **than the least of all the peoples?**
But God has chosen you because the LORD loves you
and has kept the oath that he swore to our ancestors.

**For the LORD has redeemed us with his mighty hand
and brought us out from the house of slavery.**
Know therefore that the LORD is God, who faithfully maintains
covenant loyalty with those who love him and keep his commandments.
**Surely God is faithful to a thousand generations,
but repays in their own person those who reject him.**

OPENING PRAYER

Glorious are you, O LORD, more majestic than the everlasting mountains.
We give you thanks, O God, for you are holy and your name is near. You
are known in Judah, and your name is great in Israel. Let your abode be
established forever in Jerusalem, and your dwelling place in Zion. From
the heavens you utter your righteous decrees! Let the whole earth be
astonished at what you have done, and may all your people tell of your
wondrous deeds. For your Son, Jesus Christ, has arisen from the dead to
establish judgment and to save the oppressed of the earth. Glorious are
you, O LORD, for you are holy and your name is near!

CALL TO CONFESSION

Not from the east or from the west and not from the wilderness comes
lifting up; but it is God who executes judgment, putting down one and
raising up another. Say to the boastful, "Do not boast," and to the wicked,
"Do not lift up your horn, or speak with insolence." For the LORD has set
an appointed time when he will judge with equity. All the horns of the
wicked will be cut off, but the horns of the righteous shall be exalted. But
when the earth totters, with all its inhabitants, the LORD will keep its pillars steady. Therefore, in humility and faith, let us confess our sin before
our merciful and holy God, that we may learn to rely not on ourselves but
on God, who raises the dead.

PRAYER OF CONFESSION

**O LORD our God, you are awesome indeed! Who can stand before you
when once your anger is roused? We confess that although even your
Son Jesus Christ does nothing on his own, but only what he sees you,
our heavenly Father, doing, we have foolishly gone our own way, living
disconnected, self-directed lives. You have called us to be a holy people,
yet we have not conducted ourselves as your treasured possession. We**

have been quick to covet lifeless images and slow to put away false gods. We have allowed ourselves to be ensnared by worldly things that you detest, while you have done everything necessary to set us free. Forgive us, LORD, for we have merited your anger and deserve death, yet we pray for mercy and life. Speak once more through your beloved Son, give us grace and strength to stand in his glorious presence and to honor him as is his due. For you have raised Christ Jesus from the dead, and we long to hear his voice, that we too might pass from death to life, in Jesus' holy name.

DECLARATION OF FORGIVENESS

Blessed be the God and Father of our Lord Jesus Christ, the Father of mercies and the God of all consolation! For he who has raised the crucified Savior has, in so doing, rescued us from the deadly peril of sin and its power. He is our sure hope. As the sufferings of Christ are abundant for us, so also our consolation is abundant through Christ. For in Christ every one of God's promises is a "Yes," and through Christ we say "Amen" to the glory of God, who has forgiven and established us in Christ and has anointed and sealed us by giving us his Holy Spirit in our hearts as a first installment and a guarantee of eternal life. Therefore, we will rejoice forever and sing praises to God the Father, God the Son, and God the Holy Spirit, one God, now and forever.

Resurrection Evening

Exodus 34:29–34 OR Deuteronomy 9:8–21

Psalm 75 OR Psalm 76

John 20:19–29

2 Corinthians 3:7–11 (4:16–5:1) 5:2–5 (6–10) OR Revelation 1:8–20

CALL TO WORSHIP

Not from the east or from the west
and not from the wilderness comes lifting up;
> **but it is God who executes judgment,**
> **putting down one and lifting up another.**
But I will rejoice forever;
I will sing praises to the God of Jacob.
> **We give thanks to you, O God;**
> **we give thanks; your name is near.**
People tell of your wondrous deeds,
for you indeed are awesome!
> **Glorious are you, more majestic**
> **than the everlasting mountains.**
Let all who are around him bring gifts
to the one who is awesome,
> **who cuts off the spirit of princes,**
> **who inspires fear in the kings of the earth.**

OPENING PRAYER

Our risen Lord Jesus Christ, Word of God and Son of Man, you died in
the fulfillment of the old covenant, and in your resurrection, your greater
glory outshines all that has gone before. Your voice is like the rushing

97

waters; your face is brighter than the shining sun; the sword of your mouth reveals eternal truth with the sound of a mighty trumpet. Your ministry of justification abounds in glory, gives courage and joyful endurance to the saints of your kingdom, and fills us with your Holy Spirit. Come near, Lord Jesus, and speak anew your life-giving testimony, that we may be refined, refreshed, and inspired to sing and proclaim the revelation of your glory. Alleluia! Amen!

Call to Confession

"I am the Alpha and the Omega," says the Lord God, who is and who was and who is to come, the Almighty. "At the set time that I appoint I will judge with equity. I say to the boastful, 'Do not boast,' and to the wicked, 'Do not lift up your horn on high, or speak with insolent neck.' All the horns of the wicked I will cut off, but the horns of the righteous shall be exalted." Friends, let us no longer groan under the burden of sin, but let us direct to God our longing for our heavenly dwelling. For while we are still in this tent, we wish not to be unclothed but to be further clothed, so that what is mortal—sin and death itself—may be swallowed up by life. Let us turn from our sin and confess to God our need for forgiveness, redemption, and the new life in Christ.

Prayer of Confession

O Lord our God, we confess that we your people have provoked you with our stubbornness, from the time you first gave the stone tablets of the old covenant even until now. Immersed in a culture of corrupting images, we are quick to forget your word and turn from your way. Even the good news of the resurrection and the promise of your new covenant seem too good for our hearts and minds to grasp, for in our doubt and weakness we find ourselves trusting in what our eyes can see and our hands can touch, rather than in the truth of your love and the love of your truth that your Spirit would kindle in our hearts. Forgive us, O God, for all the sin and evil we have committed, for all the doubts we have expressed, for every careless word we have spoken. Do not retain the sins of any, but forgive us in your generous and gracious mercy, that we might be truly free, and free to render you the worship and service that you rightly deserve. For you, O Christ, our crucified and risen

Savior, are our Lord and our God, and we would testify to those who have not yet seen you, that they might believe in you and be blessed.

DECLARATION OF FORGIVENESS

Do not be afraid, says the Lord Jesus. I am the first and the last, and the living one. I was dead, and see, I am alive forever and ever; and I have the keys of Death and of Hades. When the earth totters, with all its inhabitants, it is I who keep its pillars steady. From the heavens, God has uttered his judgment; the earth feared and was still when God rose up to establish his righteousness in Christ Jesus, to save all the oppressed of the earth. For if the law, the ministry of death once chiseled on stone tablets, came in a glory that is now set aside, how much more, now that Christ Jesus has defeated death, will the ministry of the Spirit come in glory? He who has prepared us for this very thing is God, who has given us the Spirit as a guarantee. Friends, believe in the good news of the gospel: in Jesus Christ, your sins are forgiven and you are free to share in his resurrection to eternal life.

Second Sunday of Easter

Hosea 14:1–9

Psalm 64 OR 119:73–96

John 16:16–24

2 Corinthians 1:23—2:17

CALL TO WORSHIP

The LORD says, "What have I to do with idols?
It is I who answer and look after you."
> The ways of the LORD are right, and the upright walk in them,
> but transgressors stumble in them.

"I am like an evergreen cypress; your faithfulness comes from me.
The wise understand these things; the discerning know them."
> Let the righteous rejoice and take refuge in the LORD.
> Let all the upright in heart glory.

"You have pain now, but it will soon turn to joy; I will see you again,
and your hearts will rejoice, and no one will take your joy from you."
> Thanks be to God, who in Christ leads us in triumphal procession,
> and through us spreads the fragrance that comes from knowing him.

OPENING PRAYER

O LORD, who exists forever! Your word is firmly fixed in heaven, and your hands have fashioned each of your children. Your faithfulness endures to all generations; you have established the earth and it stands fast, for all things are your servants. Give us understanding that we may learn your commandments, for they are enduring and are exceedingly broad. Let those who fear you see your people and rejoice, for we are yours and we hope in your word alone. Yet our souls languish for your presence and your salvation, our eyes fail with watching for your promise, as we pray that doors would be opened for you—the doors of homes and of human hearts—that we might yet speak to others as persons of sincerity, sent by you and standing in the presence of Christ, and that, as you cause others to hope in your word, our joy and yours may at last be complete. This we ask in Jesus' name.

CALL TO CONFESSION

Who has not a seen a limit to all human perfection? But the commandments of the LORD are exceedingly broad! Return, therefore, to the LORD your God, for all have stumbled because of their iniquity. Return to the LORD, and say to him, "Take away all our guilt," and do not again regard as gods the work of human hands.

PRAYER OF CONFESSION

We know, O LORD, your judgments are right, and in faithfulness you have let us be humbled. We confess that we have whet our tongues like swords, and aimed bitter words like arrows. We have often thought what we should have said to those who have hurt us, and lashed out in fear, regardless of the fact that we must someday answer to you for every careless word we have uttered. Forgive us, LORD, and help us forgive others fully, that we may not hold onto any anger or bitterness, that we may not give voice to or be outwitted by any spirit of accusation or condemnation. Let us never again bring dishonor to your name, but let your steadfast love become our comfort according to your promise through your risen Son Jesus Christ. Let your mercy come to us, that we may live, and may your Word and your Spirit ever be our joy and delight.

DECLARATION OF FORGIVENESS [Hosea 14:4–7]

Thus says the LORD,
"I will heal their disloyalty;
I will love them freely,
for my anger has turned from them.
I will be like the dew to Israel;
he shall blossom like the lily,
he shall strike root like the forests of Lebanon.

His shoots shall spread out;
his beauty shall be like the olive tree,
and his fragrance like that of Lebanon.
They shall again live beneath my shadow,
they shall flourish as a garden;
they shall blossom like the vine,
their fragrance shall be like the wine of Lebanon."
Friends, hear and believe and be at peace,
knowing that through the grace of Jesus Christ,
you are forgiven.

Third Sunday of Easter

Zechariah 13:1–9

Psalm 60 or Psalm 108

John 16:25–33

2 Corinthians 6:11—7:1

CALL TO WORSHIP

My heart is steadfast, O God, my heart is steadfast;
I will sing and make melody.
> **Awake, my soul! Awake, O harp and lyre!**
> **I will awake the dawn.**
I will give thanks to you, O LORD, among the peoples,
and I will sing praises to you among the nations.
> **For your steadfast love is higher than the heavens,**
> **and your faithfulness reaches to the clouds.**
Give victory with your right hand, and answer us,
so that those whom you love may be rescued.
> **Be exalted, O God, above the heavens,**
> **and let your glory be over all the earth.**

OPENING PRAYER

O God our Father, whose love for us we have seen and known in Christ Jesus, we thank you for sending your Son into the world, for Christ has overcome the world for the vindication of your holy name and for the salvation of all who love and believe in him. We praise you for the promise that, though we face persecution in the world, we may take heart and find peace in Jesus Christ, who has won for us the victory, and through whom we can approach you in confidence, in his name.

CALL TO CONFESSION

The LORD has spoken: "A fountain shall be opened for the house of David and the inhabitants of Jerusalem, to cleanse them from sin and impurity. On that day, I will cut off the names of the idols from the land, so that they shall be remembered no more; and also I will remove from the land the false prophets and the unclean spirit." For what partnership is there between righteousness and lawlessness? Or what fellowship is there between light and darkness? What agreement has the temple of God with idols? For we are the temple of the living God . . . Therefore, "Come out from them and touch nothing unclean," says the LORD. "Then I will welcome you, and I will be your father, and you shall be my children," says the LORD Almighty. Since we have these promises, let us cleanse ourselves from every defilement of body and of spirit, making holiness perfect in the fear of the LORD.

PRAYER OF CONFESSION [Adapted from Psalms 60 and 108]

O God, our defenses are broken, cracked, and tottering. You have caused the land to quake and have torn it open, for, we confess, we have treasured many unclean things. Therefore, you have made your people suffer hardship, and given us a cup to drink that has made us reel. Have you not rejected us, O God? Where is your Spirit to give us help, your presence to grant success against the foe? You are right to be angry at our sins; now forgive and restore us! Set up your banner for those who fear you so that we may to rally to it out of range of the enemy, for human help is worthless! Revive us, O God, for with you we shall do valiantly; you alone are able to tread down the powers that oppose your reign on this earth. This we ask in Jesus' name.

DECLARATION OF FORGIVENESS

The LORD of hosts has said of his Son, who has borne the punishment for human sin, "Strike the shepherd, that the sheep may be scattered." "In the whole land," says the LORD, "two-thirds shall be cut off and one-third left alive. And I will put this third into the fire, refine them as one refines silver, and test them as gold is tested. They will call on my name, and I will answer them. I will say, 'They are my people'; and they will say, 'The LORD is our God.'" Therefore, let there be no restriction in your affections, but open wide your hearts to the L ORD, your Redeemer, who has tried and tested and forgiven you, and given you the victory in Christ Jesus.

Fourth Sunday of Easter

Genesis 38:1–30 OR Ecclesiastes 5:1–20

Psalm 10

Matthew 22:23–33 OR Mark 12:18–27 (OR Luke 20:27–40)

2 Corinthians 7:2–16

CALL TO WORSHIP

Guard your steps when you go to the house of God!
For God is in heaven, and you upon earth; therefore let your words be few.
> **To draw near to listen is better than the sacrifice offered by fools.**
> **For they do not know how to keep from doing evil.**
Never speak rashly, nor let your heart be quick to utter a word before God.
But the LORD will hear the desire of the meek;
> **he will strengthen their hearts,**
> **and incline his ear to do justice.**
Rise up, O LORD! Lift up your hand!
Do not forget the orphan and the oppressed.
> **Those who strike terror shall perish from the land.**
> **The LORD is king forever and ever!**

OPENING PRAYER

Holy LORD, you are the God of the living, not the dead! For you, the God of Abraham, the God of Isaac, the God of Jacob, spoke from the burning bush about our ancestors, and spoke of them as living with you! Truly, you are the God of the Resurrection! Yours is the power, revealed in your Word, by which the dead are raised to new life, and Christ Jesus your Son is the head of your new creation! By your grace, you have given us the Spirit of your risen Son to dwell in our hearts, that we might die to sin and self and live together with Christ in your eternal presence! This, O LORD, is our great consolation, and by this promise, you give us joy to see us through every temporary affliction! Therefore, we draw near to you, to offer you our thanks and praise! Come, LORD, and receive our humble yet exultant testimony to your goodness!

CALL TO CONFESSION

Why do the wicked renounce God, and think in their hearts that he will not call them to account? But the LORD sees and takes notice of every cause of trouble and grief. Indeed, the Word of God distinguishes between worldly grief that produces death, and godly grief that produces a repentance that leads to salvation and brings no regret. Such godly grief is marked by earnestness, zeal, eagerness, and a longing for a clear conscience. With such godly grief at the sins of the world, let us confess our own sins, casting our burdens upon the LORD, for he will sustain us and will never permit the righteous to be moved.

PRAYER OF CONFESSION

O God, holy and merciful, we confess that we often speak before we think, giving voice to pride, skepticism, and words without knowledge. We have allowed our mouths to lead us into sin and failed to fulfill many oaths and promises. Forgive us, LORD. Do not be angry at our words. For as we came into the world, so we shall go again—naked, taking nothing with us for our toil. Therefore, search our hearts and reveal to us everything you find displeasing in your sight. Guide us into purity of thought, word, deed, and desire. Let Christ Jesus reign in each heart, that only pure thoughts and pure speech might be found among us, words spoken in love and faith and hope in the power of your Holy Spirit and in the sure promise of the resurrection.

DECLARATION OF FORGIVENESS

The judgments of the LORD are on high, yet the wicked cannot see them. As for you, receive the consolation of God! The LORD has greater confidence in you than you have in yourselves, for he knows the purposes for which he has created and redeemed you. In the end, those who trust in him and follow him earnestly will be raised in glory, like the angels of heaven. Therefore, let nothing in this world dissuade you from seeking the will of God for your life. Love him and trust him with all your heart, and let your zeal for his people be evident to all. Know that in Christ you are forgiven and set free from sin—free to make a fresh start in the life of faith.

Fifth Sunday of Easter

1 Samuel 21:1–15 OR 2 Kings 4:38–44

Psalm 49

Matthew 15:29–39; 16:1–12 OR Mark 8:1–26

2 Corinthians 8:1–6 (7–15) 16–24

CALL TO WORSHIP [see Psalm 49]

Hear this, all you peoples; give ear, all inhabitants of the world,
both low and high, rich and poor together.
> When we look at the wise, they die;
> fool and dolt perish together
> and leave their wealth to others.

Though in their lifetime they count themselves happy, they will go
to the company of their ancestors, who will never again see the light.
> Mortals cannot abide in their pomp;
> they are like the animals that perish.

For when they die they carry nothing away;
their wealth does not go down after them.
> The foolhardy are pleased with their lot,
> but God alone can ransom the soul from death,
> and Christ has done it!

OPENING PRAYER

Praise be to you, O God of Israel, for sending your only Son, Jesus Christ,
into the world to cure the sick and to restore to life those long dead.
Showing us your great compassion, Christ Jesus feeds the hungry, makes
the mute to speak, the lame to walk, the blind to see, and the maimed to
be made whole. He himself, once dead and buried, was raised to eternal

life, and thus fulfilled the sign of Jonah. Now reigning with you and the Holy Spirit in glory, he comes with the dawn to receive the worship of those who are baptized in his name, those who long for his glorious appearing. Therefore, let nothing worldly weigh down our words, our songs, our hearts, our spirits, but come and receive, O triune God, the thanksgiving and praise that is due you! Praise be to you, O God of Israel, for you alone are worthy of praise.

CALL TO CONFESSION

Truly, no ransom avails for one's life; there is no price one can give to God for it. For the ransom of life is costly, and can never suffice, that one should live on forever and never see the grave. Yet a ransom has been paid, one that is fully sufficient to supply salvation and redemption for those who find themselves convicted of sin. Therefore, let not your hearts be hardened to the reality of sin, to the full recognition of the human condition before the holy God, to your own need for grace, or to the need of your neighbor, but in humility and faith, let us confess our sins to God.

PRAYER OF CONFESSION

How slow we are, O Living Bread, to trust in you to provide in abundance! How slow to seek and to partake of the only bread that matters: the bread of your holy presence! Fearing a shortfall, we ask for signs and forecasts of better days ahead. Yet we have failed to perceive your plenteous provision by which we have not only enough to eat and some to share, but we also have some left over. Forgive us, Lord, for the sin of selfishness, for the little faith we have shown. Help us learn anew, or perhaps for the first time, the abundant joy that comes with giving, the wealth of generosity that overflows from you when we ourselves are generous. For we have too often taken for granted the privilege of sharing in your ministry to the saints, and we would give ourselves to you that we might not shrivel in fear, but excel in everything—in love, in faith, in speech, in knowledge, in utmost eagerness, and in the joy of Christian giving.

DECLARATION OF FORGIVENESS

You know the generous act of our Lord Jesus Christ, that though he was rich, yet for your sakes he became poor, so that by his poverty you might become rich. What reason have you to fear, then, in times of trouble, when iniquity and persecution surround you, when those who trust in their wealth boast of the abundance of their riches? Their graves are their homes forever, but as for you, trust in the Lord, who has given you the victory! Let your love be genuine, eager, and earnest! Let your lives be marked with the good, clear, and godly intent that characterizes those who see everything clearly in the light of Christ! For though the world is wasting away, you are forgiven, and in this grace God offers you new life and purpose. Receive it in this moment and praise the Lord!

Sixth Sunday of Easter

Deuteronomy 15:1–18 OR 19:15–21

Psalm 129

Matthew 18:1–14 (15–20) OR Luke 9:46–50; 17:1–4

2 Corinthians 9

CALL TO WORSHIP

The blessing of the LORD be upon you! He scatters abroad,
he gives to the poor; his righteousness endures forever!
The one who sows sparingly will also reap sparingly,
but the one who sows bountifully will also reap bountifully.
God loves a cheerful giver! He is able to provide every blessing in abundance,
so that, by always having enough, you may share in every good work.
Let us glorify God by obeying the confession of the gospel of Christ
and by our generous sharing in the surpassing grace of God!
May the LORD your God bless you in all that you do! For he who supplies
seed to the sower will supply and multiply the seed for sowing.
He who supplies our bread for food will grow a harvest
of righteousness. We bless you in the name of the LORD!

OPENING PRAYER

O God our Father, you have said through your Son that unless we change
and become like children, we will never enter the kingdom of heaven.
Yet you have also promised that whoever welcomes a child in your name
welcomes Christ Jesus your Son, and whoever welcomes Christ welcomes
you, who sent him into the world! Therefore, as we invoke your name and
invite you into our midst, help us be childlike and humble before you.
And further, help us welcome your children into this place, for Jesus has

said that in heaven their angels continually see your face. Truly, they are among the greatest in the kingdom of heaven, and you, the greatest of all, are among them!

CALL TO CONFESSION

Purge the evil from your midst! Occasions for stumbling are bound to come, but woe to the one who causes another to stumble! And whatever causes you to stumble, throw it away! For it is better for you to enter life maimed or lame than to be whole and thrown into the eternal fire. Whatever you bind on earth will be bound in heaven, and whatever you loose on earth will be loosed in heaven. But the Lord would have you be free from sin! Therefore, let us confess our sins to God.

PRAYER OF CONFESSION

Gracious God, you have rightly said that there will always those who are in need on the earth. Yet, you have also commanded us to open our hands to the poor, that there should be no one in need among us; and in this way we will be recognized as blessed, as your own favored people. You have made your will known that we should lend freely to many, but never borrow; yet we have become deeply indebted, spending beyond our means and binding ourselves to other masters. Forgive us, O Lord! For you are aware of our inner thoughts. You know when we are giving and when we are grudging; when we are eager and zealous to obey you, and when we are hard-hearted, tightfisted, and mean. Forgive us, merciful God, for failing to show mercy as we should, for every selfish act, for every hostile thought. We have incurred guilt, and we would learn anew, from your great generosity, to produce an overflowing harvest of thanksgiving to you! This we ask in the name of Jesus.

DECLARATION OF FORGIVENESS

The LORD's remission has been proclaimed! He is righteous and he has cut his people free from the cords of the wicked. Remember that you too were once a slave in Egypt, but the LORD your God redeemed you! As the Spirit of Christ has said in the psalm, "The plowers plowed on my back; they made their furrows long." Christ has born the stripes for our healing and forgiveness. Now, therefore, if another disciple sins, a rebuke is in order, but if there is repentance, you must forgive. If the same person sins against you seven times a day, turns back to you seven times, and says, "I repent," you must forgive. The Lord's determination to reconcile and re-store all things is such that he will leave the ninety-nine and go in search of the one that went astray. And if he finds that one, he rejoices more over the one than over the ninety-nine that never went astray. So it is not the will of your heavenly Father that even one of his little ones should be lost. Know that you are forgiven, and be at peace.

Ascension (Thursday)

Proverbs 1:1–7

Psalm 119:145–76

Mark 12:35–37 OR Luke 20:41–47

1 John 2:3–29

CALL TO WORSHIP

Let the wise hear and gain in learning.
Let the discerning acquire skill.
> **For fools despise wisdom and instruction,**
> **but the fear of the LORD is the beginning of knowledge.**
Let those who fear the LORD await the Holy Spirit,
that they may come to understand proverbs and figures, words of insight.
> **We shall delight in the words of our Savior,**
> **the Messiah, the Son of David.**
For David himself, by the Holy Spirit,
calls his own son "Lord," saying,
> **"The LORD said to my LORD,**
> **'Sit at my right hand, until I put your enemies under your feet.'"**
Let those who fear the LORD seek the Holy Spirit,
that they may gain instruction in wisdom and righteousness,
justice and equity.
> **Then we shall teach discernment to the simple,**
> **the knowledge of the LORD and prudence to the young.**

OPENING PRAYER

Hear us, O God, our heavenly Father, for you are altogether righteous!
Surely everyone who does what is right has been born of your will and

your Spirit, and those who do your will shall live forever. Come, Lord Jesus, for you are the Christ, the Son of David and the Son of the living God, and we would abide in you, so that when you are revealed we may have confidence and not be put to shame at your coming. Come, Holy Spirit! For your anointing abides in us, and with you as our teacher, we need no other. For since you teach us all things needful, and your teaching is true, we ask you to descend upon us and remain with us, instructing, inspiring, and sanctifying us, that we may in turn remain in you, abiding in our holy and righteous triune God.

CALL TO CONFESSION

Whoever says, "I have come to know Christ," but does not obey his commandments, is a liar, and in such a person the truth does not exist. Whoever says, "I am in the light," while hating a brother or sister or another believer, is still in the darkness, walks in the darkness, and does not know the way to go, because the darkness has brought on blindness. Do not love the world or the things in the world. The love of the Father is not in those who love the world; for all that is in the world—the desire of the flesh, the desire of the eyes, the pride in riches—comes not from the Father but from the world. And the world and its desire are passing away. Children, it is the last hour! As you have heard that antichrist is coming, so now many antichrists have come. From this we know that it is the last hour. Who is the liar but the one who denies that Jesus is the Christ? This is the antichrist, the one who denies the Father and the Son. But no one who denies the Son has the Father. Such warnings concern those who would deceive God's elect, but let us not be deceived about sin and righteousness and judgment; rather, let us confess our sin to the One who has already defeated it, that we might be free to abide forever in his truth and love.

PRAYER OF CONFESSION [Psalm 119:145a, 146–49, 153–56, 158–60, 176]

With my whole heart I cry;
answer me, O LORD.

> I cry to you; save me,
> that I may observe your decrees.

I rise before dawn and cry for help;
I put my hope in your words.

My eyes are awake before each watch of the night,
that I may meditate on your promise.
In your steadfast love hear my voice;
O LORD, in your justice preserve my life.
Look on my misery and rescue me.
Plead my cause and redeem me;
give me life according to your promise.
Salvation is far from the wicked,
for they do not seek your statutes.
Great is your mercy, O LORD;
give me life according to your justice.
I look at the faithless with disgust,
because they do not keep your commands.
Consider how I love your precepts;
preserve my life according to your steadfast love.
The sum of your word is truth;
and every one of your righteous ordinances endures forever.
I have gone astray like a lost sheep; seek out your servant,
for I do not forget your commandments.

DECLARATION OF FORGIVENESS

Rest assured, old and young, children of God of every age, for you know the Father who is from the beginning; in Christ you have conquered the evil one, and your sins are forgiven in Jesus' name. Therefore, be strong in faith, for the word of God abides in you. Whoever says, "I abide in him," ought to walk just as he walked. Whoever loves a brother or sister lives in the light, and in such a person there is no cause for stumbling. Now by this we may be sure that we know him, if we obey his commandments, for whoever obeys his word, truly in this person the love of God has reached perfection. Beloved, to love God and one another is no new commandment, but an old commandment that you have had from the beginning; the old commandment is the word that you have heard. Yet it is ever new and it is true in him and true in you, because the darkness is passing away and the true light is already shining. Everyone who confesses Jesus as the Son of God has the Father also. Therefore, let what you heard from the beginning abide in you. If what you heard from the beginning abides in you, then you will abide in the Son and in the Father. And this is what he has promised us: eternal life. Thanks be to God!

Seventh Sunday of Easter

Jeremiah 9:23–24; 24:1–10

Psalm 115

Mark 11:27–33 [AND Mark 12:35–37 if Ascension is not observed]
OR Luke 20:1–8 [AND Luke 20:41–47 if Ascension is not observed]

2 Corinthians 10

CALL TO WORSHIP

The heavens are the LORD's heavens,
but the earth he has given to human beings.
> Not to us, O LORD, not to us, but to your name give glory,
> for the sake of your steadfast love and your faithfulness.
You who fear the LORD, trust in the LORD!
He is our help and our shield.
> The LORD has been mindful of us; he will bless us;
> he will bless those who fear the LORD, both small and great.
Our God is in the heavens; he does whatever he pleases.
May the LORD give you increase, both you and your children.
> We will bless the LORD from this time on and forevermore.
> Praise the LORD!

OPENING PRAYER

Christ Jesus our Savior, you who are seated at the right hand of God and whose enemies will soon become a footstool for your feet, even King David calls you "Lord"! All authority belongs to you, and you, in turn, have authorized your disciples to build and to plant, to pray for an increase of faith, to hope for an enlarged sphere of action in which to reach out with the good news of your kingdom! Therefore, draw near and instruct us in your ways, that we might no longer live according to human standards, but discern the fields that God has assigned to us and proclaim your good news in lands both far and near, for the honor of your holy name, and for the glory of the Father and of the Holy Spirit, with whom you reign as one God, both now and forever!

CALL TO CONFESSION

Those who measure and compare themselves against others do not show good sense. It is not those who commend themselves that are approved, but those whom the Lord commends. Those who manufacture and trust in idols are like the idols themselves. They have mouths, but do not speak; eyes, but do not see. They have ears, but do not hear; noses, but do not smell. They have hands, but do not feel; feet, but do not walk; they make no sound in their throats. Therefore, let no one make an idol, whether of himself or for himself! But of those who cry out to the LORD, the God of Israel says, "I will build them up, and not tear them down; I will plant them, and not pluck them up. I will give them a heart to know that I am the LORD; and they shall be my people and I will be their God, for they shall return to me with their whole heart."

PRAYER OF CONFESSION

Almighty God, we live among a generation that constantly questions authority. We confess that we too have been slow to heed your messengers, to acknowledge the authority of your Word and your Spirit, to believe and obey the gospel of your Son, our Sovereign, Jesus Christ. We have too often feared human opinions more than your holy judgments. Forgive us, LORD, for our rebellion and for the bad fruit we have borne. Make us new by the transforming power and grace of your Spirit, that we might gain victory over the forces that have bound us, and bear good and lasting fruit for the kingdom of your beloved Son, in whose holy name we pray.

DECLARATION OF FORGIVENESS

Thus says the LORD: Let not the wise boast in their wisdom, the mighty boast in their might, or the wealthy boast in their wealth; but let those who boast, boast in this, that they understand and know me, that I am the LORD; I act with steadfast love, justice, and righteousness in the earth, for in these things I delight, says the LORD. Consider Jesus Christ, the Son of God, who, being meek and gentle, did not wage war according to human standards, but had divine power to destroy strongholds. He it is who brings down the proud who raise themselves up against the knowledge of God. But you, who are now ransomed and redeemed in Christ, must take every thought captive for obedience to Christ, who by his power and authority has set you free. I declare to you in the name of Jesus Christ, you are forgiven.

Pentecost Sunday

Exodus 4:1–17 OR Deuteronomy 5:1–15 (6–21) 22–33 OR 31:23–29 OR
Daniel 12:1–13

Psalm 119:113–36

Matthew 10:9–23 OR Luke 12:1–12

2 Corinthians 11:1—12:1

CALL TO WORSHIP

The LORD has spoken with a loud voice
from the fire, the cloud, and the thick darkness!
> **Who has heard the voice of the living God speaking,**
> **and remained alive?**
Truly the LORD is holy and greatly to be feared!
Yet, just as truly, God may speak to someone and the person may still live.
> **O LORD, show us your greatness and glory!**
> **Let us hear your voice from the fire!**
The LORD has said: If only they had such a mind as this,
to fear me and to keep my commandments always,
that it might go well with them and their children forever!
> **Let us draw near and hear what the LORD our God will say.**
> **Let us listen and do all that the LORD commands.**

OPENING PRAYER

O LORD our God, who gave power to Moses to perform signs and wonders, who gives speech to mortals by the Holy Spirit, long ago you made
a covenant with all who are here and alive today, when you spoke face to
face with our ancestors at the holy mountain! Renew us, we pray, in that
covenant of grace! For we live like sheep amidst a generation of wolves.

Pour out your Holy Spirit upon us! Fill us with your wisdom and teach us what to say. Give us courage to acknowledge you before others and inspiration to testify to Jesus Christ your Son, that he will in turn acknowledge us before the angels of God! Instruct us anew as your trusting and obedient children to observe your statutes and ordinances, for we know that when we turn neither to the right nor to the left, but follow the path that you have commanded, it will go well, and we shall live long in this land that you have given us to possess. Yes, fill us with the fullness of your Holy Spirit, that those with whom we share your glorious gospel may believe that you are the LORD, the God of our ancestors, the God of Abraham, the God of Isaac, and the God of Jacob, the God and Father of our Lord Jesus Christ, in whose name we pray.

CALL TO CONFESSION

Beware of being double-minded and hypocritical. Nothing is covered up that will not be uncovered; nothing is secret that will not become known. What you have said in the dark will be heard in the light, and whatever you have whispered behind closed doors will be proclaimed from the housetops. Do not fear those who kill the body, and after that can do nothing more. But fear the one who has authority to cast into the fire. For the law of the Lord has been broken. Indeed, it is a witness against our rebellious and stubborn ways, and in time the Lord will judge! Therefore, let us lament that God's law is not kept. Let us learn to hate every false way and direct our steps according to the truth.

PRAYER OF CONFESSION

Eternal God, holy and righteous, your church has been promised in marriage as a chaste virgin bride to one husband, your Son, Jesus Christ. Yet, as Eve by the serpent was deceived, so we too have been led astray from a sincere and pure devotion to Christ. You are right to feel divine jealousy, for there are those who proclaim other gospels than the one gospel of Jesus Christ, those who speak in other spirits than the Holy Spirit, and indeed we, as well as the church of which we are a part, have submitted to these and become accommodated all too readily. You spurn all who go astray from your statutes; for their cunning is in vain. Yet, your decrees are wonderful; therefore, mindful of our weakness and sin, we now long for your commandments and thirst for your

saving Spirit. Make our steps steady according to your promise, and never again let iniquity have dominion over us. Uphold your penitent people according to your promise, that we may live and thrive in your presence. Let not our hope in you be put to shame. Our eyes fail from watching for your salvation, and for the fulfillment of your righteous promise. Deal with your servants according to your steadfast love, and give us understanding. Make your face shine upon us, and teach us the way to eternal life in Jesus Christ.

DECLARATION OF FORGIVENESS

Blessed be our Lord and Savior Jesus Christ, the Son of God, for Christ is our hiding place and our shield, and we have hope in him who is the Living Word of God. The unfolding of his words gives light; it imparts understanding to the simple. The least little sparrow is not forgotten in God's sight, and even the hairs of your head are all counted. Therefore, do not be afraid, for you are of more value than many sparrows. The Lord is gracious to all those who love his name. Though there will be times of suffering, and in the end a time of anguish, such as has never occurred since nations were born, yet at that time you shall be delivered, everyone who is found written in the book of life. Many of those who sleep in the dust of the earth shall awake, some to everlasting life, and some to shame and everlasting contempt. But those who are wise shall shine like the brightness of the sky, and those who lead many to righteousness, like the stars forever and ever. Many shall be purified, cleansed, and refined, but the wicked shall continue to act wickedly. None of the wicked shall understand, but those who are wise shall understand. Happy are those who persevere, for the one who endures to the end will be saved and shall rise for the reward at the end of days. Blessed be the Lord forever!

PART III

Ordinary Time (Propers 4–29)
Trinity—All Saints'—Christ the King

Trinity Sunday

1 Kings 9:1–9; 11:1–13 OR Ecclesiastes 8:1–17

Psalm 35

John 15:18–25 (26–27); 16:1–4a

2 Corinthians 12:11–21; 13:1–10 (11–13)

CALL TO WORSHIP

Contend, O LORD, with those who contend with your servant!
Take hold of shield and buckler, and rise to our aid!
> O LORD, who is like you? For you deliver the weak from those
> too strong for them, the needy from those who despoil them.
Draw the spear and javelin against my pursuers.
Say to my soul, "I am your salvation."
> Then my soul shall rejoice in the LORD,
> exulting in his deliverance!
You have seen, O LORD; do not be silent! O LORD, do not be far from me!
Wake up! Bestir yourself for my defense, my God and my LORD!
> Let those who desire my vindication shout for joy, be glad, and say,
> "Great is the LORD, who delights in the welfare of his people."

OPENING PRAYER

Almighty Father, your Son, Jesus Christ, is our Savior and Lord, yet he has
also graciously called us his friends, for he has made known everything
that he has heard from you. He has chosen and appointed us to go and
bear fruit, fruit that will last, and has promised that you, our heavenly
Father, will give whatever we ask in his name. Christ Jesus, Son of the
Father, you have commanded us to abide in your love and to love one
another. Spirit of truth, sent from the Father, you testify on behalf of Jesus

Christ, and you empower us to testify as well, and to bear the fruit of the Spirit. Now, therefore, God the Father, God the Son, and God the Holy Spirit, grant that we may be free from the world that does not know you. Consecrate this house that you have built, that your name and your glory may reside here. Watch over this place and all who worship you here; let your heart be near to us as we draw near to you. Help us walk uprightly and with integrity of heart, doing according to all that you have commanded. Keep us from stumbling. Let us never turn aside from following you, but rather, let your kingdom, your glorious reign, be established over this place and over all who enter here, now and forever. This we ask in Jesus' name, with the full assurance that you will do this for you glory.

CALL TO CONFESSION

Examine yourselves to see whether you are living in the faith. Test yourselves. For Jesus Christ is in you, unless, of course, you fail to meet the test! The servant is not greater than the master. If the world persecuted the Son of God, the world will not leave the followers of Jesus untouched. If Christ had not come and spoken to the world, the world would not have sin; but now there is no excuse for sin. If Jesus had not done the works that no one else did, the world would not have sin. But now the world has seen and hated both the Son of God and the heavenly Father. This was to fulfill the word that is written in the law: "They hated me without a cause." But because the sentence against evil is not executed speedily, the human heart is prone to do evil. Though sinners do evil a hundred times and prolong their lives, yet it will be well with those who fear God, because they stand in awe before him, but it will not be well with the wicked, neither will they prolong their days, because they do not fear God. Therefore, in the fear of the LORD, let us confess our sin.

PRAYER OF CONFESSION

Holy, holy, holy LORD, God of power and might, we confess that we have seen and participated in a vanity that takes place on the earth by which the righteous are treated as wicked, and the wicked are treated as though they were righteous. Even among those whom you have called to be your church there is quarreling, jealousy, anger, selfishness, slander, gossip, conceit, disorder, impurity, immorality, and licentiousness. Slow to repent of past sins, we now humble ourselves before you. We are as those who lament for a dying mother; we are bowed down and in mourning. Forgive us, O God, for the wrongs we have done, both personally and as your people in this world. Let those who would rejoice at the failings of your church be put to shame and confusion. Rescue us from the ravages of lying and tempting spirits! Set us anew upon the straight and narrow path, O God of righteousness. Then we will thank you in the great congregation; in the mighty throng we will praise you. Vindicate your people, O LORD, according to your grace. Then we shall tell of your righteousness and sing your praises all day long!

DECLARATION OF FORGIVENESS

The Lord Jesus Christ is not weak in dealing with you, but is powerful in you. For though he was crucified in weakness, he lives by the power of God; and though we too are weak in him, yet we will live with him, also by the power of God. Therefore, let everything be done for the sake of building up one another in faith, in truth, in love. Do nothing wrong, but do what is right, for those who walk the way of Christ cannot do anything against the truth, but only for the truth, as they grow in the love and the Spirit of Christ toward perfection. Know, then, that by the grace of Jesus Christ you are forgiven, and free to persevere in faith.

Proper 4
Ordinary Time 9 / May 29–June 4 *(if after Trinity)*

Deuteronomy 31:30—32:27 OR Isaiah 5:8–17

Psalm 142

Matthew 17:9–20 OR Mark 9:9–29 OR Luke 9:18–27 (28–36) 37–45

Philippians 2:14–30

CALL TO WORSHIP

Give ear, O heavens, and I will speak.
Let the earth hear the words of my mouth.
> **May your words drop like rain, your speech condense like dew;**
> **like gentle rain on the grass, like showers on new shoots.**
When the Most High apportioned the nations and divided humankind,
he fixed the boundaries of all the peoples, choosing Israel as his own.
> **Let us proclaim the name of the LORD**
> **and ascribe greatness to our God!**
He sustained them in the wilderness, in a howling desert waste.
He shielded and cared for them; he guarded Israel as the apple of his eye.
> **As the eagle spreads its wings and bears its young aloft,**
> **the LORD alone guided him, with no help from a foreign god.**

OPENING PRAYER

O God, our Provider, who sent the Son of Man to suffer for human sin
and raised him from the dead by your almighty mercy, draw near and fill
us with your Holy Spirit, increasing the faith of all who would receive you.
For though we believe, O LORD, yet we would have you help our unbelief!
Speak to us and remind us of your amazing miracles and your wonderful deeds! Raise us up, we pray. Lead us into such height and depth and

breadth of faith that we might, in faith, remove the mountains that would intimidate us and block our progress on the everlasting way, for you have promised us, as your disciples, that if we only have faith like a mustard seed, nothing will be impossible for us. Come, LORD, that we may worship you and enjoy your holy presence, find refreshment in your Word and Spirit, and be equipped for the work of Christ, for his name's sake and yours.

CALL TO CONFESSION

The work of God our Rock is perfect, and all his ways are just. He is a faithful God, just and upright and without deceit! Yet his children have dealt falsely with him, in every perverse and crooked generation. Remember the days of old, consider the years long past; ask your ancestors, and they will inform you; your elders, and they will testify. They too made him jealous and provoked him with strange gods. They sacrificed, not to God, but to deities they had never known, and they scoffed at the Rock of their salvation. Is this how we should repay the LORD, as foolish and senseless people? Surely not! For God is our Creator, our Father and Maker. But learn and be mindful of the Rock that bore you. Do not forgot the God who gave you birth. Let us draw near to God and confess our sins.

PRAYER OF CONFESSION

Merciful God, hear us as we confess our troubles, our laments, and our sins. For when our spirits are faint, you know the way. In the paths where we walk there are many hidden traps and snares. Give heed to our cry, for we are brought very low. Our past sins and fears and failures of faith are known to you, yet we long to be free of them. Lead us out of bondage and gloom, that we may give thanks to your holy name. Save us from every evil and temptation, for the forces that oppose us are too strong for us to overcome them on our own. We have no refuge, no portion, but in you. Therefore, absolve us and cleanse us of every stain. Then we will know we are at home among the righteous, when you have dealt bountifully and mercifully with your people. This we ask in Jesus' name.

DECLARATION OF FORGIVENESS

Hear and hold fast to the word of life, by which you shall boast in the day of Christ that you have not run or labored in vain! For though we live amidst a crooked and perverse generation, yet God has shown us great mercy! Christ has poured himself out as a libation for you, a sacrifice to God and an offering of faith. The work that Christ has done for you makes you blameless and innocent, a child of God without blemish. Therefore, rejoice and be of good cheer! Do all things without murmuring, arguing, or complaining, but let your light shine like stars in the world! Seek your own interests no longer, but those of Jesus Christ and of the family of faith. Forgive one another as God has forgiven you. Welcome and honor one another with joy in the LORD and the power of faith.

Proper 5
Ordinary Time 10 / June 5–11 (*if after Trinity*)

Deuteronomy 32:28–47 OR Isaiah 5:18–24

Psalm 74

Matthew 12:22–37 OR Luke 11:14–23

1 John (3:8–15) 4:1–6

CALL TO WORSHIP

Praise the LORD, O heavens! Worship him, all you gods!
For he will repay those who hate him, and cleanse the land for his people.
> **Rise up, O God, plead your cause.**
> **Remember how the impious scoff all day long.**
The LORD says, "See now that I, even I, am he; there is no god besides me.
I kill and I make alive; I wound and heal;
and none can deliver from my hand."
> **Do not forget the clamor of your foes,**
> **the uproar of your adversaries that rages on and on.**
Take to heart the words of the LORD, for they will testify about you.
Teach them to your children as commandments to be kept.
> **This is no trifling matter, but it is to be our very way of life.**
> **Thus may we live long in the land the LORD has given us to possess.**

OPENING PRAYER

Our LORD Jesus Christ, you who came in the flesh and who, by the power of the Holy Spirit, cured the sick and drove out the spirits of darkness, come to us and grant each of us an awareness of your holy presence, and with it the gift of spiritual discernment. For in you we have the victory over sin, deception, and error; in you, who have overcome the world, we too shall overcome, for you who are in us are greater than the one who is in the world. Come, LORD Jesus, Son of David, Son of God! We are gathered in your name.

CALL TO CONFESSION

God has said of those who reject him and willfully persist in sin: "They are a nation devoid of sense; there is no understanding in them. If they were wise, they would understand this; they would discern what the end would be. How could one have routed a thousand, and two put a myriad to flight, unless their Rock had sold them, the LORD had given them up? . . . Where are their gods, . . . who ate the fat of their sacrifices and drank the wine of their libations? Let them rise up and help you, let them be your protection!" Yet, of the enemies of his people, the LORD says, "Vengeance is mine, for the time when their foot shall slip; because the day of their calamity is at hand, their doom comes swiftly." Indeed, Scripture promises, "the LORD will vindicate his people, and have compassion on his servants, when he sees that their power is gone, neither bond nor free remaining." Since we are powerless to save ourselves from the power of sin which is the law, and from the wages of sin, which is death, let us confess our sins.

PRAYER OF CONFESSION

As you have said, O Lord, it is out of the abundance of the heart that the mouth speaks; you have warned that on the day of judgment, we will have to account for every careless word we have uttered. Even now, O Lord, many of our words ring their condemnation in our ears. Mindful of that coming day, we approach you in confession, asking mercy and absolution for the ways in which we have harbored many thoughts and spoken many words that displease you and reveal the content of our hearts. Forgive us, O Lord, for though it is the house of the enemy that is known by its division, we have allowed disunity to undermine your church and sin to separate us from you. Yet, we long to be with you, not against you; we desire only to join you in gathering the lost to you; we have no desire to see your sheep scattered. Guard us, we pray, against the sins of thought, word, and deed, and keep us especially from the sin against the Holy Spirit. For it is by the Spirit of God that your Son came, casting out demons and thereby manifesting your sovereignty on earth. Truly, O God our King, you are from of old, working salvation in the earth! You divided the sea by your might, crushed the head of the serpent, and gave him as food to the wild beasts. But do not deliver the soul of your dove to them; do not forget how we need you, O God. Have regard for your covenant, for the dark places of the land are full of violence. Do not let your downtrodden be put to shame, but lift us up that we may praise your name.

DECLARATION OF FORGIVENESS

The LORD does not cast off forever, but he has sent Jesus Christ, come in the flesh, full of grace and the spirit of truth. Indeed, Christ himself is the Truth who exposes every falsehood. Do not believe everything you hear, but test the spirits to see whether they are from God. By this you know the Spirit of God: every spirit that confesses that Jesus Christ has come in the flesh is from God, and every spirit that does not confess Jesus is not from God. Therefore, tend to your life, test your thoughts, and choose you words with care, the same care you would show to a newly planted tree. Do everything in your power to make the tree good, and its fruit will be good. Refine your life so that, when you open your storehouse, you will produce good treasure, shining truth, worthy words. But have nothing to do with the evil practices that you see at work in the world around you. Little children, you are from God, and in Christ the Victor, you have already overcome the world; for the one who is in you is greater than the one who is in the world.

Proper 6
Ordinary Time 11 / June 12–18 (*if after Trinity*)

Isaiah 6:8–13 OR Ezekiel 17:22–24 OR 31:1–18 OR Daniel 4:1–37

Psalm 7

Matthew 13:10–17 (18–33) 34–35 OR Mark 4:1–25 OR Luke 8:4–25; 13:18–21

Ephesians 4:17–25 (4:26–5:1–2) 5:3–7 OR 2Peter 2:1–22

CALL TO WORSHIP [Psalm 14]

O LORD my God, in you I take refuge!
Save me from all my pursuers, and deliver me!
> Let the assembly of the peoples be gathered around you,
> and over it take your seat on high.
O let the evil of the wicked come to an end, but establish the righteous,
you who test the minds and hearts, O righteous God.
> God is my shield, who saves the upright in heart.
> God is a righteous judge, who has indignation every day.
If one does not repent, God will whet his sword;
he has bent and strung his bow, making his arrows fiery shafts.
> I will give to the LORD the thanks due to his righteousness,
> and sing praise to the name of the LORD Most High.

OPENING PRAYER

Let us bless the Most High! Let us praise and honor the one who lives forever. How great are his signs, how mighty his wonders! For your sovereignty, O LORD, is everlasting, and your kingdom endures from generation to generation. All the inhabitants of the earth are as nothing. You are able to do whatever you desire with the host of heaven and with those

136

who live upon the earth. Who can stay your hand or say to you, "What are you doing?" Let us praise, extol, and honor the High King of heaven, for all his works are truth, and his ways are justice; and he is able to bring low those who walk in pride.

Call to Confession

The Spirit of the Lord has spoken, saying: You must no longer live as the unbelievers live, in the futility of their minds. They are darkened in their understanding, alienated from the life of God because of their ignorance and hardness of heart. They have lost all sensitivity and have abandoned themselves to licentiousness, greedy to practice every kind of impurity. That is not the way you learned Christ! For you were taught to put away your former way of life, your old self, corrupt and deluded by its lusts, to be renewed in the spirit of your minds, and to clothe yourselves with the new self, created according to the likeness of God in true righteousness and holiness. So then, putting away falsehood, let all of us speak the truth, for truth is in Jesus, and we are members of one another. Let us confess our sins.

Prayer of Confession

O God our Father, you sent your Son, your holy seed, into the world, speaking parables and proclaiming what had been hidden from the foundation of the world. Yet, we confess, though we have heard much, we have listened little; though we have seen much, we have perceived little. Our hearts have grown dull, and our ears are hard of hearing; we have often shut our eyes, and in doing so, denied ourselves the healing that you would give us, if we were simply to turn to you. So now we turn to you, in earnest, asking your forgiveness. May we never again shy away from the narrow gate, or be like the newly washed sow that soon trots off to wallow in the mud. Let not your word be snatched from our hearts, neither let it be rootless or choked by the cares, the riches, and the pleasures of the world. Help us endure in times of testing and pay attention to how we listen to and receive you, for we have had enough, more than enough of our dullness, deafness, and sin, and we would have your kingdom come among us; we would have your Son, Jesus Christ, reign over us, no longer concealed in parables, but manifest and glorified, for every eye to see.

Declaration of Forgiveness

Hear the good news! The LORD knows how to rescue the godly from trial. In Christ Jesus, the holy seed, God has spoken, and he will accomplish his redeeming purpose for those who trust in him. What is more, he has revealed to you the secrets of the kingdom of heaven! Blessed are you who have heard the truth and received it! For to those who have, more will be given, and they will have an abundance; but from those who have nothing, even what they have will be taken away. Therefore, live as those in whom the good seed has been sown, as those who, having heard the word, now hold it fast in an honest and good heart and bear fruit with patient endurance. Let your light shine so that others may see it. Let no greed or impurity of any kind even be mentioned among you, as is proper among the saints. Entirely out of place is obscene, silly, and vulgar talk; but instead, let there be thanksgiving! For though no impure person, or one who is greedy (that is, an idolater), will have any inheritance in the kingdom of Christ and of God, you who belong to Christ stand to share in his inheritance with him and with all the saints who have been forgiven, re-created, and redeemed. Praise the LORD!

Proper 7
Ordinary Time 12 / June 19–25 (*if after Trinity*)

Isaiah 29:1–24 OR Isaiah 59:1–21

Psalm 55

Matthew 15:1–20 OR Mark 7:1–20

1 Timothy 4

CALL TO WORSHIP

In an instant, suddenly, the LORD of hosts will visit you,
with thunder, earthquake, wind and tempest, the flame of a devouring fire.
God is enthroned from of old. He hears and humbles
those who do not change, those who do not fear the LORD.
The nations that fight against Mount Zion shall vanish like a dream.
Your foes shall be like fine dust, the multitude of tyrants
like chaff in the wind.
O that I had wings like a dove! I would fly away and be at rest,
taking shelter in the wilderness from the wind and tempest.
The LORD has said: I will once again do amazing things
with this people, shocking and amazing!
The wisdom of the wise shall perish; discernment shall be concealed.
Then you shall speak from out of the earth,
your words from deep underground.

OPENING PRAYER

Gracious God, you have created everything good, to be received with thanksgiving and sanctified by your word and by prayer. Your Son has even declared all foods clean, which you created to be received with grateful hearts by those who believe in and know Christ Jesus as the Truth.

Now, therefore, send your Holy Spirit into our hearts and nourish us with the words of the faith and sound teaching. Direct, O LORD, our training in godliness, not only for this life but also for the life to come. For we have set our hope on you, the living God, the Savior of all those who believe. This we ask in Jesus' name.

CALL TO CONFESSION

The Spirit has warned through the Scriptures that in later times some will renounce the faith by listening to lies and deceit, giving in to hypocrisy with an impaired conscience. They will make void the word of God and abandon his commandment, in order to pass on human traditions. As the prophet said, "This people honors me with their lips, but their hearts are far from me; in vain do they worship me, teaching human precepts as doctrines." When we replace God's word with our empty human words, we defile ourselves, for it is what comes out of a person that defiles. On the other hand, "every plant that the heavenly Father has not planted will be uprooted." God will do away with human wisdom and conceal human discernment, so that his people should be nourished with his own words of faith and eternal life. Let us then believe the LORD and what he is about to do, for though all have sinned, those who believe God are reckoned as righteousness. Therefore, cast your burden on the LORD, and he will sustain you; he will never permit the righteous to be moved.

PRAYER OF CONFESSION

Our Holy and Gracious God, we confess that we have often seen things upside down. We have made a habit of following blind guides rather than fully trusting in your Word, and have risked falling into the Pit. We confess that we have been afraid to see what you would show us, to hear what you would say to us; thus, we find ourselves in a stupor, in a spirit of deep sleep. We have forgotten ourselves and foolishly regarded you, the potter, as though you were the clay; we have rashly questioned why you have made us this way. Forgive us, LORD! Give ear to our prayer, and do not hide yourself from our supplications. For we are besieged and hemmed in by sin. Redeem us unharmed from the battles we wage, for many forces and foes are arrayed against us. Nevertheless, we will trust in you to hear us as we call upon you, to save us from the wages of sin, and train us up in godliness. We pray in Jesus' name.

DECLARATION OF FORGIVENESS

The LORD has spoken: In a very little while the fruitful field will be regarded as a forest. On that day the deaf shall hear the words of a scroll, and out of their gloom and darkness the eyes of the blind shall see. The meek shall obtain fresh joy in the LORD, and the needy shall exult in the Holy One of Israel. No longer shall Jacob be ashamed, no longer shall his face grow pale. For when he sees his children, the work of the LORD's hands, in his midst, they will sanctify the name of the Holy One of Jacob, and will stand in awe of the God of Israel. And those who err in spirit will come to understanding, and those who grumble will accept instruction. Now, therefore, as God's chosen and forgiven, set one another an example in speech and conduct, in love, in faith, in purity. Give your attention to the reading of Scripture and to sound doctrine. Do not neglect the gifts that have been given you, but put these things into practice with devotion, so that others may see your progress. Pay close attention to yourself and to what you say; for in doing so, you may effect the salvation of others. Receive the good news of forgiveness with thanksgiving, for in Jesus Christ, we are forgiven.

Proper 8
Ordinary Time 13 / June 26–July 2

2 Kings 20:1–21 OR Amos 4:1–3 OR Malachi 3:6–18 (4:1–6)

Psalm 56

Matthew 9:27–34 OR John 5:31–47

1 Corinthians 3:12–15 (3:16–4:5) 4:6–21 OR 2 John

CALL TO WORSHIP

May grace, mercy, and peace be with us from God the Father
and from Jesus Christ, the Father's Son, in truth and love.
> Let our service to God and our faith in Christ Jesus
> be a spectacle to the world, to angels and to mortals.
If we are fools for the sake of Christ, let others become wise in him.
If we are weak, may they become strong.
> When reviled, we shall bless; when persecuted, we shall endure;
> when slandered, we shall speak kindly.
For even if we are like the rubbish of the world, the dregs of all things,
we know that the LORD himself has received as much from the world.
> Therefore, in God, whose word I praise, in God I trust;
> I am not afraid; what can flesh do to me?
My vows to you I must perform, O God;
I will render thank offerings to you.
> For you have delivered my soul from death,
> and my feet from falling,
> so that I may walk before you in the light of life.

Opening Prayer

Lord God Most High, your prophets, your Word, and your works all testify to your Son, our Savior, in whom we have received the promise of eternal life. He whom you sent in the power of your Spirit is the one whom we preach, and beyond whose teaching we must not venture, for truly he has revealed all things needful for life, salvation, and peace. Even if the world holds us in disrepute, let us take comfort and find shelter in you, Father, Son, and Holy Spirit, as we offer you worship in your sanctuary and in your holy presence, in which we have the assurance of your merciful and powerful kingdom.

Call to Confession

Thus says the Lord of hosts: I the Lord do not change; therefore you, my children, have not perished. Ever since the days of your ancestors you have turned aside from my statutes and have not kept them. Return to me, and I will return to you, says the Lord of hosts. . . . Those who revere the Lord shall be mine, says the Lord of hosts, and those who consider my name shall be my special possession on the day when I act, and I will spare them as parents spare their children who serve them. Then once more you shall see the difference between the righteous and the wicked, between one who serves God and one who does not. Friends, let us confess our sin and disobedience to our gracious, merciful, and holy God.

Prayer of Confession

Sovereign Lord, we confess that often we miss the point of your many witnesses. Some of us make more of the written word than of your Son, the Living Word to whom it testifies. Others go beyond what is written, beyond the teaching of Christ, and lose sight entirely of your new creation, your revealed promise, and your powerful kingdom. One way or another, sin clouds our vision, selfishness distracts us from your will, and pride undermines the loyal service we would render you. Forgive us, Lord, and restore to us a right and proper devotion to your Son, that your Word might abide in us and we in him, and when the Day discloses our work, we will most assuredly be saved and the works that you have given us to do may prove to be endowed with your Spirit.

DECLARATION OF FORGIVENESS

Friends, rest assured, God is merciful to those who confess their sins and gracious to those who are penitent; he deals with those who trust in him with love in a spirit of gentleness, and even keeps count of our tears. This we know, that God is for us, opening our eyes to his sovereign ways, and giving us his truth to abide in us and be with us forever. Therefore, be not afraid, but love one another and let your joy be complete as you walk each day in the truth of the gospel: in Jesus Christ we are forgiven. Alleluia! Amen!

Proper 9
Ordinary Time 14 / July 3–9

2 Kings 6:8–23

Psalm 57 OR 3

Matthew 12:38–50 OR Luke 11:24–36

1 Corinthians 5:1–5 (6–8) 9–13; 6:1–11

CALL TO WORSHIP [from Psalm 3]

O LORD, how many are my foes! Many are rising against me;
many are saying to me, "There is no help for you in God."
> **But you, O LORD, are a shield around me,**
> **my glory, and the one who lifts up my head.**
I cry aloud to the LORD, and he answers me from his holy hill.
I lie down and sleep; I wake again, for the LORD sustains me.
> **I am not afraid of ten thousands of people**
> **who have set themselves against me all around.**
Rise up, O LORD!
Deliver me, O my God!
> **Deliverance belongs to the LORD!**
> **May your blessing be on your people!**

OPENING PRAYER

O LORD our refuge, you have spoken through your prophets and your teachers of wisdom, yet you are among us as one greater still! You have expanded our understanding of family, instructing us that whoever does the will of our heavenly Father is a brother or sister of Jesus Christ the Son. Yet one far greater than the church is here! Yes, you are here, for you have promised to be present in the Spirit where your followers are gathered in your name, you who were three days in the heart of the earth and are now seated at the right hand of power. Therefore, awaken us to the nearness of your presence, speak to us with the power of our risen Lord Jesus, and give us courage and determination to obey, for we are eager to receive the blessing you promised when you said, "Blessed are those who hear the word of God and obey it!"

CALL TO CONFESSION

Your eye is the lamp of your body. If your eye is healthy, your whole body is full of light; but if it is not healthy, your body is full of darkness. Therefore, consider whether the light in you is not darkness. How, for instance, do you view your fellow believers? Does any one among you have a grievance against another? Do you not know that the saints will judge the world? Do you not know that we are to judge angels—to say nothing of ordinary matters? But, to have unsettled disputes with one another is already a defeat. Why not rather be wronged, as Jesus was, who was rejected by the world and put to death for sins he did not commit? Why not rather be defrauded? Do you not know that wrongdoers will not inherit the kingdom of God? But let us put our houses in order, and rid ourselves of everything unclean, by confessing our sins.

PRAYER OF CONFESSION

O LORD our God, the Father of lights, forgive us, we pray, for harboring darkness in our hearts and minds, for seeking signs other than the unsurpassed sign that you have given: the Son of Man, the Son of God, risen from the dead! Almighty God, you have said that an evil and adulterous generation asks for other signs. How foolish we have been to forget the greatest sign of all, to fail to receive the wonderful news that, as Christ is raised from the dead, we, too, when we take shelter in him, are free from sin and victorious over death! Therefore, we ask your mercy as one, knowing that you desire us to be one in Christ: Be merciful to me, O God, be merciful and forgive, for in you my soul takes refuge; my soul takes refuge in the shadow of your wings, until the destroying storms pass by. Send from heaven and save me; send forth your steadfast love and faithfulness, for I have sinned against you and I stand in constant need of your grace. Remove all darkness from me and let me be filled with the light of Christ forever, in Jesus' holy name.

DECLARATION OF FORGIVENESS

Do not be afraid, but hear the good news! You have been forgiven, washed, sanctified, and justified in the name of the LORD Jesus Christ and in the Spirit of our God. For our paschal lamb, Jesus Christ, has been sacrificed, once and for all. Therefore, conduct yourselves as persons of sincerity, that in the day of Christ you may be pure and blameless. And let your light shine before others that they may see your good works and give thanks to your Father in heaven. No one after lighting a lamp puts it in a cellar, but on a lampstand so that those who enter may see the light. If then your whole body is full of light, with no part of it in darkness, it will be as full of light as when a lamp gives you light with its rays. In this way, the LORD will fulfill his purpose for you, for those whom he has forgiven and redeemed in Jesus Christ.

Proper 10
Ordinary Time 15 / July 10–16

Jeremiah 7:1–15 OR Daniel 2:1–49

Psalm 17:8–14 (15) OR 83

Matthew 24:1–8 (OR Mark 13:1–8)

1 Corinthians 7:1–40

CALL TO WORSHIP [Psalms 17:8–10, 13; 83:1, 18; 17:15]

Guard me as the apple of the eye;
hide me in the shadow of your wings,
> **from the wicked who despoil me,**
> **my deadly enemies who surround me.**

They close their hearts to pity;
with their mouths they speak arrogantly.
Rise up, O LORD, confront them, overthrow them!
> **By your sword deliver my life from the wicked,**
> **from mortals—by your hand, O LORD—**
> **from mortals whose portion in life is in this world.**

O God, do not keep silence;
do not hold your peace or be still, O God!
> **Let them know that you alone,**
> **whose name is the LORD,**
> **are the Most High over all the earth.**

As for me, I shall behold your face in righteousness;
> **when I awake I shall be satisfied, beholding your likeness.**

OPENING PRAYER [see Daniel 2:20–23, 47]

Blessed be your name, O God, from age to age, for wisdom and power are yours! Truly, you are God of gods and Lord of kings and a revealer of mysteries! You change times and seasons, depose and establish rulers, give wisdom to the wise, and knowledge to the understanding. You reveal deep and hidden things; you know what is in the darkness, and light dwells with you. To you, O God of our ancestors, we give thanks and praise, for you give your faithful ones wisdom and power, and reveal yourself to those who seek you. Draw near to us now, we pray, as we gather in your presence to magnify your holy name.

CALL TO CONFESSION [Jeremiah 7:2–7]

"Hear the word of the LORD, all you people . . . , you that enter these gates to worship the LORD. Thus says the LORD of hosts, the God of Israel: Amend your ways and your doings, and let me dwell with you in this place. Do not trust in these deceptive words: 'This is the temple of the LORD, the temple of the LORD, the temple of the LORD.' For if you truly amend your ways and your doings, if you truly act justly one with another . . . and if you do not go after other gods to your own hurt, then I will dwell with you in this place, in the land that I gave of old to your ancestors forever and ever." In penitence and faith, let us seek the abiding presence and mercy of the LORD, by confessing our sins to God.

PRAYER OF CONFESSION

Holy and eternal God, your promises are sure and your words are trustworthy and true. Yet we confess that we have been taken in by deceptive words, borne the burden of needless worry, harbored fears that have alienated others, and nursed anxieties that have undermined our faith. You have spoken to us persistently, but we have not listened; you have called to us, but we, your church, have refused to hear you. Merciful God, forgive us; do not cast us from your sight. Grant us courage, wisdom, and a willing spirit, to repent of past sins and not return to them again, to wait upon you to fulfill your Word, and to do so watchfully and with unfailing faith in Jesus Christ our LORD, in whose name we pray.

Declaration of Forgiveness

When Jesus spoke of the birth pangs that would presage his return, he said, "Do not be alarmed." And when Paul wrote to the Corinthians, saying, "the appointed time has grown short," and "the present form of this world is passing away," he also said, "be free from anxieties," for "it is to peace that God has called you." For the gospel truth is that the kingdom of Christ, Jesus' reign of grace and forgiveness, is spreading through all the earth, and it is for this reason he has come: to set you free for life under his heavenly and holy sovereignty. Therefore, be at peace, and "let each of you lead the life that the LORD has assigned, to which God has called you"; indeed, "from now on, let those who deal with the world live as though they had no dealings with it." For in Jesus Christ, you are forgiven and free to live a life unencumbered by the cares of this world.

≪ *The Apocalyptic Discourse* ≫

Proper 11
Ordinary Time 16 / July 17–23

Deuteronomy 31:23–29 OR Micah 7:1–7 OR Daniel (11:40–45) 12:1–13

Psalm 54

Matthew 10:17–22a; 24:9–14 OR Mark 13:9–13

1 Corinthians 9:1–15

CALL TO WORSHIP [Psalm 54]

Save me, O God, by your name,
and vindicate me by your might.
> **Hear my prayer, O God;**
> **give ear to the words of my mouth.**
For the insolent have risen against me, the ruthless seek my life;
they do not set God before them.
> **But surely, God is my helper;**
> **the LORD is the upholder of my life.**
He will repay my enemies for their evil.
In your faithfulness, put an end to them.
> **With a freewill offering I will sacrifice to you;**
> **I will give thanks to your name, O LORD, for it is good.**
For he has delivered me from every trouble,
> **and my eye has looked in triumph on my enemies.**

OPENING PRAYER

O LORD our protector, we live in troubled times, when many run to and fro in pursuit of vain things, and lawlessness increases. Nevertheless, in Jesus Christ you deliver your people from death to life, everyone who is found written in your book of life. Speak to us once more of eternal things: of life and love, of your holy splendor and your complete joy, that we may gain wisdom and shine with your glory like the brightness of the sky, like the stars forever and ever. This we ask in the name of your Son and our Lord, Jesus Christ, the Sun of Righteousness.

CALL TO CONFESSION [Micah 7:2–4, 7]

Hear the word of the LORD through the prophet Micah: The faithful have disappeared from the land, and there is no one left who is upright. Their hands are skilled to do evil, and the powerful dictate what they desire. The best of them is like a brier, the most upright of them a thorn hedge. The day of their sentinels, of their punishment, has come; now their confusion is at hand. But as for me, I will look to the LORD, I will wait for the God of my salvation; my God will hear me. Let us confess our sins to God, with hope and confidence in his mercy.

PRAYER OF CONFESSION

Holy and righteous God, your law testifies against us, for we have been a rebellious and stubborn people. Heaven and earth have witnessed how often we have turned aside from the way that you have commanded us to follow. Troubles have befallen your church and this nation, because of what we and our ancestors have done, and have failed to do, in your sight. Have mercy upon us, we pray, for we have no other hope than in your grace, and no other claim to righteousness than that which Jesus Christ imparts to us by means of your Holy Spirit. Forgive us thoroughly, O LORD, that we may be purified, cleansed, and refined; and help us go forth proclaiming the gospel of forgiveness, that we may share in its blessings with our Savior and your Son, in whose name we pray.

DECLARATION OF FORGIVENESS

Thus says the LORD: Be strong and bold, for I will be with you. Put no obstacle in the way of the gospel of Christ. But let the good news go forth, free of charge, and let it be proclaimed to all nations that in Jesus Christ, you are forgiven. Happy are those who persevere in faith, trusting in this good news, until the end. Know that Christ Jesus has redeemed you from sin and death, and be at peace.

⚔ *The Apocalyptic Discourse* ⚕

Proper 12
Ordinary Time 17 / July 24–30

Deuteronomy 4:32–40 OR Isaiah 65:10–65 OR Ezekiel 7: (1–9) 10–27
OR Zechariah 14: (1–3) 4–9 (10–21)
Psalm 50: (7–8) 9–21 (22–23) OR 105: (1–6) 12–15, 26–36 (37, 43–45)
Matthew 24:15–22 OR Mark 13:14–20 OR Luke 21:20–24
1 Corinthians 10: (14–17) 18–11:1

CALL TO WORSHIP [see Deuteronomy 4:32–40]

Ask now about former ages, long before your own,
ask from one end of heaven to the other:
has anything so great as this ever happened
or has its like ever been heard of?
> Has anyone ever heard the voice of a god
> speaking out of a fire, as you have heard, and lived?
Has any god ever attempted to take a nation for himself
from the midst of another nation,
by a mighty hand, an outstretched arm, and terrifying displays of power,
as the LORD your God did for you in Egypt before your very eyes?
But to you it was shown, so that you would acknowledge:
> the LORD is God; there is no other besides him!
And because he loved your ancestors, he chose their descendants after them.
He brought you out of Egypt with his own presence, by his great power,
driving out nations greater and mightier than yourselves,
and bringing you in, giving you their land for a possession, as it is still today.
So acknowledge today and take to heart:
> the LORD is God in heaven above
> and on the earth below; there is no other.

Opening Prayer

O Lord our God, Lord of heaven and earth, your prophets foretell a day, a continuous day, when at evening there shall be light, when living water shall flow out from Jerusalem, and when you yourself will come, with all your holy ones, and stand on the Mount of Olives; it is a day known only to you, when you shall be acknowledged Sovereign over all the earth. Give us patience and perseverance, we pray, to look forward to that day with faith, not fear, with hope, not despair. For though that day will come in the wake of great suffering, you have mercifully set a limit to it, for the sake of your elect; and you are gracious to come even into our midst in the present moment, on this very day of the Lord, that we might receive you as our Lord, that we might know you better and be known by you, even as we are known in the world to belong to you. Therefore, we pray, come, Lord Jesus. Come, Holy Spirit. Raise up your people and empower our worship, that we might give due thanks and praise to our heavenly Father, with whom you reign eternally, one God, now and forever.

Call to Confession

The Lord God has promised: My servants shall eat and drink, they shall rejoice and sing for gladness of heart. But those who forsake the Lord are destined for hunger and thirst, for sword and slaughter, for pain of heart and anguish of spirit. Therefore, let us examine ourselves: Have we provoked the Lord to jealousy? Do we think more of fate and destiny, do we have more fear of demons than of the living and holy God who alone can save? Silver and gold cannot save on the day of the wrath of the Lord. But the sacrifice that God desires is a sacrifice of thanksgiving. Let us openly confess our sins and thus render right worship to the God who shows us steadfast love, and who summons us to himself, saying, "Call on me in the day of trouble; I will deliver you, and you shall glorify me."

Prayer of Confession

Holy and merciful God, we confess that we have acted wickedly. We have forgotten your words, cast off discipline, and spoken against those whom you love. We all too quickly assume that you are just like us, that we know your mind, that we may speak judgment against others with impunity. Forgive us, O Lord, for we have too often forgotten how far you have come and how much you have done to save us from death,

depravity, and despair. We have neglected to pay our vows to you, to whom we have promised lifelong loyalty. Cleanse us from every sin, forgive our every transgression, wash us thoroughly in the blood of the Lamb, our Lord Jesus Christ, and receive once again our sacrifice of thanks and praise. This we ask in his name.

DECLARATION OF FORGIVENESS

The LORD speaks: Sharon shall become a pasture for flocks, and the Valley of Achor a place for herds to lie down, for my people who have sought me. Then whoever invokes a blessing in the land shall bless by the God of faithfulness, and whoever takes an oath in the land shall swear by the God of faithfulness; because the former troubles are forgotten and are hidden from my sight. Indeed, since for your sake the LORD has cut short the times of greatest suffering, consider yourself free from fear, free to seek not your own advantage but that of the other, free to do everything for the glory of God, whose purpose in sending Jesus Christ into the world was and is to save the world. Know that you are forgiven, that your future is securely in the hands of God, and be at peace.

Proper 13
Ordinary Time 18 / July 31–August 6

Genesis 19:1–29

Psalm 59

Matthew 24:23–35 (36–44) OR Luke 17:20–37

1 John 2:3–29 OR 2 John OR 2 Peter 2:1–22

CALL TO WORSHIP [Matthew 24:30–31; Psalm 59:9, 16–17]

The sign of the Son of Man will appear in heaven,
and all the tribes of the earth will mourn,
and they will see "the Son of Man coming on the clouds of heaven"
with power and great glory.
> **And he will send out his angels with a loud trumpet call,**
> **and they will gather his elect from the four winds,**
> **from one end of heaven to the other.**
O my strength, I will watch for you;
for you, O God, are my fortress.
> **I will sing of your might;**
> **I will sing of your steadfast love in the morning.**
For you have been a fortress for me
and a refuge in the day of my distress.
O my strength, I will sing praises to you,
> **for you, O God, are my fortress,**
> **the God who shows me steadfast love.**

OPENING PRAYER

Rouse yourself, LORD God of hosts. Come, for the sake of your steadfast love. For you alone are God and your words will never pass away. The world and its desires are passing away, but you have sent your Son Jesus Christ in the flesh to redeem your people from the snares of the world. Send him once again, we pray, who is at the very gates, to save us from this evil generation, from every lying spirit, from those who are bloodthirsty and who treacherously plot evil. Deliver us, O God. Rescue those who love you, who hope in Christ, who remain in his love and abide in his teaching; then it will be known to the ends of the earth that your kingdom rules over all, for the praise of your glory.

CALL TO CONFESSION

Surely those who abide in Christ ought to walk just as he walked and obey his commandments; and whoever loves a brother or sister lives in the light, and in such a person there is no cause for stumbling. But whoever claims to know and love the Lord, yet does not obey his commandments, is a liar, and in such a person the truth does not exist. Whoever says, "I am in the light," while hating another believer, is still in the darkness, walks in the darkness, and does not know the way to go, because the darkness has brought on spiritual blindness. Let us confess our sins together, and seek reconciliation in the light of Christ, that the love of God might be brought to perfection in us, and seen in our wholehearted love for one another.

OR

Love, in truth, is not permissiveness, but it aspires to perfection, for "whoever obeys God's word, truly in this person the love of God has reached perfection." But where destructive opinions are introduced, the way of truth is maligned, and those with unsteady souls, enticed from the way of love by the lures of licentiousness, become irrational creatures of instinct, insatiable for sin, reveling in dissipation, with eyes full of adultery and hearts trained in greed. As the proverb says, "The sow is washed only to wallow in the mud." Therefore, friends, let us turn away from every evil thought, word, and deed, that we might not suffer the penalty for wrongdoing. Rather, let us seek the merciful grace of Jesus Christ, whose commandment is love and whose name is truth, for the darkness is passing away and the true light is already shining.

PRAYER OF CONFESSION

Eternal God, our gracious Father, merciful Christ, and Holy Spirit, we confess that though you have called us to be righteous, we have often been deceived by the desire of the flesh, the desire of the eyes, and pride in riches. We have believed, and we ourselves have spoken, foolish nonsense, following false promises of freedom from those who themselves are enslaved to corruption. Where you have called us to join in your mission to this dying world, we have allowed ourselves to become entangled in its defilements. Forgive us, Lord, and set us free once again; overthrow the forces that deceive, oppress, and corrupt your creation and your church. Let the powers of heaven be shaken for the sake of your elect; only let us not look back, that we might not lose sight of your coming kingdom, your glorious reign, that is at once on its way to meet us and already here among us, in our very midst. This we ask in Jesus' name.

[Note: In the DECLARATION below, the bracketed portion may be omitted, but there may be certain circumstances, as when congregations and denominations face particularly strong spiritual or doctrinal opposition, under which this passage from 1 John 2:18–23 functions as both a word of assurance and a reinstatement to the mission of the body of Christ in the world.]

DECLARATION OF FORGIVENESS

The commandment that we have had from the beginning is this: let us love one another. And this is love: that we walk according to the Lord's commandments. And this is the joyful truth in which we walk: little children, your sins are forgiven on account of his name. Fathers and mothers, you know him who is from the beginning. Young people, in Christ you have conquered the evil one; be strong, for the word of God abides in you; in the power of his Holy Spirit, you have overcome the evil one. [Children, it is the last hour! As you have heard that antichrist is coming, so now many antichrists have come. From this we know that it is the last hour. But you have been anointed by the Holy One, and all of you have knowledge; you know the truth, and you know that no lie comes from the truth. Who is the liar but the one who denies that Jesus is the Christ? This is the antichrist, the one who denies the Father and the Son. No one who denies the Son has the Father; everyone who confesses the Son has the Father also.] Let what you heard from the beginning abide in you. If what you heard from the beginning abides in you, then you will abide in the Son and in the Father. And this is what he has promised us, eternal life. And now, little children, abide in him, so that when he is revealed we may have confidence and not be put to shame before him at his coming. Grace, mercy, and peace will be with us from God the Father and from Jesus Christ the Son, in truth and in love.

Proper 14
Ordinary Time 19 / August 7–13

Genesis 6:1–8 OR Zechariah 9:1–8 (9–12) 13–17
Psalm 37: (1–2) 12–38 (39–40)
Matthew 24: (36–44) 45–51 OR Luke 12: (35–40) 41–48
1 Corinthians 11:2–22 (23–26) 27–34

CALL TO WORSHIP

The LORD will appear and his arrow will go forth like lightning!
He will make your vindication shine like the sun,
the justice of your cause like the noonday.
> The LORD God will sound the trumpet
> and march forth in the whirlwinds at his right hand.
On that day the LORD their God will save them
for they are the flock of his people;
> like the jewels of a crown they shall shine on his land.
> For what goodness and beauty are his!
Grain shall make the young men flourish,
and new wine the young women.
> Be still before the LORD, and wait patiently for him.
> Commit your way to the LORD; trust in him, and he will act.

OPENING PRAYER

Lord Jesus Christ, we know neither the day nor the hour when you will come again to gather up your church or to stand upon the earth, but we do know that we are to remain awake, dressed and ready for action, with our lamps lit as servants awaiting the return of their Master. To think, even for a moment, that you are delayed is to risk falling asleep, and therefore, we invite you to draw near to us now, for you have promised to do so, saying, "I am with you always." Therefore, by the swift wind of your Spirit, raise our expectations, O Lord. Let no one go through the motions of worship without becoming acutely aware that you are near, indeed, that you are here, watching, waiting, examining every heart. Surely you will speak, O Lord, through the Word, written, read, and preached, and you will feed your people—you, the Christ, the living bread, you, the Holy Spirit, of whom we all partake as we drink from same spiritual drink, the spiritual rock of Christ.

Call to Confession

Do not fret because of the wicked; do not envy those who do wrong and appear to prosper, for they will soon fade like the grass, and wither like the green herb. The LORD knows that the wickedness of humankind is great in the earth; even as it was in the days of Noah, so it is in these last days. Every inclination of the human heart is only evil continually. But the LORD delights in the faith of those who long for it to be otherwise. For the LORD loves justice, and does not forsake his faithful ones. Therefore, depart from evil, and do good, examining yourselves in the light of Christ, who gave himself up for you, and by whose grace you will live eternally; indeed, you shall abide forever. In preparation for that eternal day, let us confess our sins.

Prayer of Confession

O Christ our Peace, you have warned us to refrain from anger, to forsake wrath, and to surrender worry, for it leads only to evil. Yet, we confess, our hearts are not at peace. We see much that is evil and unjust in the world, and we find ourselves reacting in ways that are not your ways, with anger and anxiety. Worst of all, we find that the evil things we despise most in the world are the very things in which we become complicit, and thus we realize many of our own thoughts, inclinations, desires, and deeds are not pleasing to you, despite our assumptions and attitudes. Forgive us, Lord. Awaken us to your nearness, and awaken in us an ever-greater desire to think and speak and act according to your will. Let any and every wicked way be removed from us, that we might wait upon you faithfully as those who shall inherit the land. For the salvation of the righteous is from you, O Lord; you are our refuge in

times of trouble. Therefore, help us, heal us, and rescue us from every evil power and influence. This we ask in your most holy name.

DECLARATION OF FORGIVENESS

When we guide our steps according to the ways of the LORD, he delights in our ways and makes our steps secure. If we stumble, we shall not fall headlong, for the LORD himself holds us by the hand. Therefore, trust in the LORD and do good, so you will live in the land, and enjoy security. Take delight in the LORD, and he will give you the desires of your heart. Be at peace and be firm in your faith in Jesus Christ, for truly the meek shall inherit the land, and delight themselves in abundant prosperity.

⋘ *Prelude to the Passion* ⋙

Proper 15
Ordinary Time 20 / August 14–20

Jeremiah 22:1–9 OR Zechariah 7:1–14

Psalm 58

Matthew 23:13–39 OR Luke 11:37–54

1 Timothy 3

CALL TO WORSHIP

Thus says the LORD of hosts: Render true judgments,
show kindness and mercy to one another.
> **Do not oppress the widow, the orphan, the alien, or the poor;**
> **and do not devise evil in your hearts against one another.**
Hold fast to the mystery of the faith with a clear conscience. When tested,
prove yourselves blameless; be serious, temperate, and faithful in all things.
> **Show great boldness in the faith that is in Christ Jesus.**
> **For the church of the living God is his household,**
> **the pillar and bulwark of the truth.**
Without any doubt, the mystery of our religion is great:
Christ was revealed in flesh, vindicated in spirit,
> **seen by angels, proclaimed among the nations,**
> **believed in throughout the world, taken up in glory!**

OPENING PRAYER

O LORD of Hosts, in your wisdom you have sent many prophets and
apostles, some of whom were killed and persecuted, to testify to your
Son; and Christ Jesus himself suffered rejection by the world and by the
very people he was sent to save. Yet, through this very rejection, you have
revealed yourself as not only despised and rejected, but as surpassingly

merciful and glorious, and you have, by condemning sin and redeeming sinners in this way, given us hope. Surely there is a reward for the righteous; surely there is a God who judges on earth! Thanks be to you, O Lord, for Christ our righteousness! Thanks be to you, O God, that when we hear the stinging words of rebuke from your Son, we may hear them with the knowledge that they proceed from love and truth, grace and faith, and they are intended for our ultimate good. Grant us, therefore, courage to hear and obey you, strength to stand in your presence, and a thorough purification of our inner being, that we may offer you true worship of which you alone, Father, Son, and Holy Spirit, are worthy!

CALL TO CONFESSION

Do you indeed judge people fairly? No, in your hearts you devise wrongs. Do not be like the wicked, who go astray from the womb; they err from their birth, speaking lies. Like the deaf adder they have stopped up their ears, so that they do not hear. But the word of the LORD puts the question to both the people and their priests: When you fast and lament, is it for me that you fast? And when you eat and drink, do you not eat and drink only for yourselves? The word of the LORD has come, but people have adamantly refused to listen, they have turned a stubborn shoulder, and covered their ears to shut out the word that the LORD has spoken through the law and the prophets. Just as, in those days, when I called they would not hear, so, when they called, I would not hear, and I scattered them with a whirlwind among all the nations that they had not known. Thus, a pleasant land was made desolate. But in these last days, God has spoken through his Son, that we might have forgiveness even long before we realize our need for it. Let us then respond to God's kindness by confessing our sins and our need for his mercy.

PRAYER OF CONFESSION

We confess we have not kept covenant with you, O LORD our God, but we have worshiped other gods and served them. We have sworn oaths casually and not kept them; we have given freely of small things, but neglected the weightier matters of justice, mercy, and faith; we have maintained outward appearances of piety, while allowing our interior lives to fester with greed, hypocrisy, and self-indulgence; though we bear the name of Christ, we have failed to live and to love as Jesus has

taught us. Thus we must confess that we have taken your name in vain. Forgive us, LORD, for by our words and actions we have stopped others from entering your kingdom, and we ourselves have failed to enter. Yet, do not let your house become desolate. Let not the passersby say to one another, "Why has the LORD dealt this way with his people?" But give us, everyone, a fresh start, and gather us under the shelter of your wings. Though we have not always been willing, we will it now! Absolve and cleanse us, O LORD, both inside and out, for we long to see you and say, "Blessed is the one who comes in the name of the LORD!"

DECLARATION OF FORGIVENESS

The vindication of Christ through his faithfulness is imparted to you by his grace. The saying is sure: In Jesus Christ, you are forgiven and set free to live according to God's will. Now, therefore, act with justice and righteousness, and do no wrong or violence to the alien, the orphan, or the widow. Be above reproach, serious, sober, respectable, hospitable, not violent but gentle, neither quarrelsome nor greedy. Raise your children to be respectful in every way—for if someone does not know how to manage his own household, how can he take care of God's church? If you will indeed obey this word, then Christ your King shall enter through the gates of God's house and shall sit upon the throne of David, and you, his saints, shall reign with him. Be at peace, and serve your God with gladness.

Proper 16
Ordinary Time 21 / August 21–27

Genesis 3:1–7 (8–21) 22–24 OR Jeremiah 8:4–13 OR 24:1–10 OR Habakkuk 3:1–19

Psalm 140

Matthew 21:12–22 OR Mark 11:12–25 (26)

Colossians 1:29–2:5 (16–19) 20–23

CALL TO WORSHIP

O LORD, I have heard of your renown,
and I stand in awe, O LORD, of your work.
> **In our own time revive it;**
> **in our own time make it known!**
Though the fig tree does not blossom, and no fruit is on the vines;
though the produce of the olive fails and the fields yield no food;
> **though the flock is cut off from the fold**
> **and there is no herd in the stalls,**
yet I will rejoice in the LORD;
I will exult in the God of my salvation.
> **God, the LORD, is my strength; he makes my feet**
> **like the feet of a deer, and makes me tread upon the heights.**

OPENING PRAYER

Come, O LORD, let your glory cover the heavens, and let the earth be filled with your praise. For your glory is brighter than the sun and your rays come forth from your hand, where your power lies hidden. Let the deep give forth its voice, as you brandish your bow and split the earth with rivers. Let the sun raise high its hands; let the moon stand still in its exalted place, at the light of your arrows speeding by, at the gleam of your flashing spear. For soon you will tread the earth in fury, in anger you will trample the nations, when you drive your horses, your chariots to victory, when you trample the sea with your horses and churn the mighty waters. Come forth, O Lord, to save your people, to rescue your anointed ones. Crush the head of the enemy, and lay his house bare from foundation to roof. Turn his own arrows against the powers that scatter your people as a whirlwind and gloat as if ready to devour the poor. Let those who fear you tremble at the sound. Let those who love you and believe your promises wait quietly for the day when your enemies are vanquished.

Call to Confession

Thus says the Lord: When people fall, do they not get up again? If they go astray, do they not turn back? Why then have my people turned away in perpetual backsliding? They have held fast to deceit, they have refused to return. I have given heed and listened, but they do not speak honestly; no one repents of wickedness, saying, "What have I done!" All of them turn to their own course, like a horse plunging headlong into battle. Even the stork in the heavens knows its times; the turtledove, swallow, and crane observe the time of their coming; but my people do not know the ordinance of the Lord. They have acted shamefully and committed abominations; yet they were not at all ashamed and did not know how to blush. Yet, even now, those who return to me with their whole heart shall be my people and I will be their God; I will set my eyes upon them for good, and I will restore them to the land. I will build them up, and not tear them down; I will plant them, and not pluck them up. I will give them a heart to know that I am the Lord. Therefore, let us wholeheartedly turn to the Lord, confessing our sin.

Prayer of Confession

O Lord our God, we confess that we have sinned as our ancestors did who first ate of the fruit of the tree of the knowledge of good and evil. By exalting ourselves, we have fallen further away through disobedience. Instead of bearing good fruit, we have hidden from you our sins and our fruitless pursuits in garments of fig leaves. We have chosen things that lead to death rather than life, and blamed one another for our own faults. We have failed to believe you with our whole hearts, and

we, your church, have replaced prayer before your heavenly throne with peddling and marketing of worldly things. Forgive us, O Christ, for you have promised that whatever we ask for in prayer with faith, we will receive. In your wrath, may you remember your mercy. O LORD, you are our God; hear our supplications, be our strong deliverer, and cover our heads in the day of battle. For we are as children, crying, "Save us! Hosanna to the Son of David!" Let our prayers that proceed from our deepest need be as praises to your ears. Then the righteous shall give thanks to your holy name, and the upright shall live in your presence. These things we ask in the name of Jesus.

DECLARATION OF FORGIVENESS

Now let your hearts be encouraged and united in love, so that you may have all the riches of assured understanding and have the knowledge of God's mystery, Christ himself, in whom are hidden all the true treasures of wisdom and knowledge. Let no one deceive you with plausible arguments. For what you have asked in faith and repentance is swiftly given by our merciful God. Rejoice at this good news, and remain firm in your faith in Christ, for in Christ you have you died with him to the rudiments and regulations of human teachings and to the elemental wisdom of the universe. You no longer belong to the world, but you belong to Jesus Christ, in whom you are truly free and freely forgiven!

Proper 17
Ordinary Time 22 / August 28–September 3

Numbers 11:1–30 OR Isaiah 45:20–25 OR Jeremiah 4:19–31 OR
Zechariah 8:1–23

Psalm 68:11–31 (32–35) OR 120

John 10:19–21 (22–30) 31–42

1 Corinthians 14:1–40

CALL TO WORSHIP

Blessed be the LORD, who daily bears us up!
God is our salvation!
> **Our God is a God of salvation,**
> **and to God, the LORD, belongs escape from death.**
Your solemn processions into the sanctuary are seen, O God my King!
Bless the LORD in the great congregation, O you who are of Israel's fountain!
> **Blessed be God forever! Summon your might, O God;**
> **show your strength, as you have done for us before.**
Sing to God, O kingdoms of the earth; listen, he sends out his mighty voice!
Sing praises to the LORD, whose power is in the skies!
> **Awesome is the LORD in his sanctuary, the God of Israel;**
> **for he gives power and strength to his people.**

OPENING PRAYER

Our Living Lord Jesus Christ, who has shown us many good works from
our heavenly Father, with whom you are One: we thank you for the gift
of eternal life, and for the assurance that we will never perish, that no
one will ever snatch us out of your hand! What blessed assurance this is!
What boldness it gives us to witness to you! Yet our vision is dim and our

hearing is dull, and those in the world to whom we would witness some-times seem to have no sense at all! Lord, open blind eyes and sharpen our vision, open deaf ears and refine our understanding, that when we hear the sound of your voice we will know it and be quick to follow! For truly, Lord, the works that you do in the Father's name testify to you, and the gifts that you have given us are encouraging indeed. Therefore, draw near, that we, your church, may praise you in the Spirit and be built up in love by your prophetic word. This we ask for your name's sake.

Call to Confession

Thus says the LORD: "Assemble yourselves and come together, draw near, you survivors of the nations! They have no knowledge—those who carry about their wooden idols, and keep on praying to a god that cannot save. Who told this long ago? Who declared it of old? Was it not I, the LORD? There is no other god besides me, a righteous God and a Savior; there is no one besides me. Yet my people are foolish, they have no understand-ing. They are skilled in doing evil, but do not know how to do good. Yet, though the whole land be a desolation, I will not make a full end. Turn to me and be saved, all the ends of the earth! For I am God, and there is no other. By myself I have sworn: only in the LORD are righteousness and strength and salvation to be found!" Friends, let us confess our sin.

Prayer of Confession

O LORD of hosts, you have commanded us to love truth and peace, but the secrets of our hearts are not hidden from you! We confess we have often given voice to complaining; rather than eagerly attending to the words of your prophets, we have often recoiled from their challenging admonitions and sought our own way. When faced with adversity, we have longed for the cold comforts of former ways, forgetting or failing to believe in your unlimited power. Forgive us, O LORD! For all things are possible with you! Yet, we also confess that, when mindful of your power and eager for your spiritual gifts, we have used them for bol-stering ourselves and causing disorder. You, however, are not a God of disorder, but of peace. Help us use our gifts for the building up of the whole church. Gracious and merciful God, set us free from former ways, through the atoning work of your beloved Son. Put your Spirit upon us, that all might have your word inside them, ready at any moment to

prophesy, console, encourage, and build up! This we ask in Jesus' name, that our confession of sin may truly become our confession of faith!

DECLARATION OF FORGIVENESS

Do not be afraid. Speak the truth to one another, render judgments that are true and that make for peace. Say to one another, "Come, let us entreat the favor of the LORD, and seek the LORD of hosts; I myself am going." Many peoples and strong nations shall come to seek the LORD in Jerusalem, and entreat the favor of the LORD. For thus says the LORD: Old men and women shall again sit in the streets of Jerusalem, with staff in hand because of their great age. And the city shall be full of children playing in the streets. Even though it seems impossible to the remnant of this people, should it also seem impossible to me, says the LORD? Thus, I will save my people from the east and from the west; and I will bring them home. They shall be my people and I will be their God, in faithfulness and in righteousness. There shall be a sowing of peace; the vine shall yield its fruit, the ground shall give its produce, and the skies shall give their dew; and I will cause the remnant of this people to possess all these things. I will save you and you shall be a blessing. Therefore, do not be afraid, but let your hands be strong, you who have been redeemed by the LORD.

Proper 18
Ordinary Time 23 / September 4–10

Exodus 28: (1–29) 30–43 OR 2 Samuel 15:30–37; 16:15–17:4
OR 2 Chronicles 30:1–27

Psalm 141

John 11:45–57

1 Corinthians 16:1–24

CALL TO WORSHIP [Psalm 141]

Come quickly, O LORD,
give ear when I call to you.
> **Let my prayers be as incense before you,**
> **and the lifting up of my hands as a sacrifice of praise.**

Set a guard over my mouth, O LORD;
keep watch over the door of my lips.
> **Do not turn my heart to any evil,**
> **to busy myself with wicked deeds.**

Let the faithful correct me. Never let the oil of the wicked anoint my head,
for my prayer is continually against their wicked deeds.
> **But my eyes are turned toward you, O GOD, my Lord;**
> **in you I seek refuge; be my rock and my sure defense.**

OPENING PRAYER

Father of lights, let your glory fill this place as it once filled the tabernacle
of the covenant; let your cloud and fire guide us on every stage of our
journey of faith, as you once guided Israel through the wilderness. Come
and reign over us; oversee our renewal, reform, and restoration. Let there
be great joy here as has not been for many generations. Bless your people

gathered here and receive our praises as we bless your name. Let our voice be heard on high, O LORD; and let our prayer come to your holy dwelling in heaven. For the sacrifice of your Son Jesus Christ, which he has made for the sins of the world, has not been in vain, but bears the fruit of faith in every tribe and people and language and nation! Therefore, come, O God, and gather all your dispersed children into one, in the name of our risen Savior and Lord, Jesus Christ!

CALL TO CONFESSION

Purify yourselves and keep the Sabbath; sanctify yourselves and seek the LORD, that he may turn again to the remnant of his people. Do not be like the faithless and the stiff-necked, but yield yourselves to the LORD, and come to his sanctuary. For as you return to the LORD, your kindred and your children will find compassion. The LORD your God is gracious and merciful, and will not turn away his face from you, if you return to him. Humble yourselves and be of one heart to do what is commanded by the word of the LORD.

PRAYER OF CONFESSION

Good and gracious Lord, pardon us for all our sins as we set our hearts to seek you. Forgive us for your name's sake, even though we have not kept your laws. Hear our cry, heal this land, and sanctify us for your service, that we may show those in need of hope the face of the redeemed. For the sins of this land have reached your ears, and we have seen with our own eyes how devastating is your wrath. Stay your hand, O Lord, by your mercies, that we might live and serve under your grace. Have compassion on us, and direct us to those who long to receive compassion and relief from their trials. Help us, in repentance and faith, to rearrange our lives in a manner that is consistent with placing you first in our hearts and minds, with worshiping you as you desire, in truth and justice and humility. This we ask for your name's sake.

DECLARATION OF FORGIVENESS

Be glad and rejoice! Be courageous and strong, keep alert and stand firm in your faith! Let all that you do be done in love, and let your spirits be refreshed in the Lord. Devote yourselves to the service of the saints, and pray that a wide door for effective work may be opened for those who would tell the good news of forgiveness that you yourselves have received. Recognize, support, and greet one another warmly in the Lord. For in the death of Christ, God has reconciled you to himself and in his resurrection, you have also been raised to new life. Have faith in the truth and know that in Christ you are forgiven and free. The grace and love of the Lord Jesus Christ be with you all.

Proper 19
Ordinary Time 24 / September 11–17

Deuteronomy 16:1–17

Psalm 92: (1–4) 5–11 (12–15)

Matthew 26:1–19 OR Mark 14:1–16 OR Luke 22:1–13

1 Timothy 5

CALL TO WORSHIP [Psalm 92]

It is good to give thanks to the LORD,
to sing praises to your name, O Most High;
    to declare your steadfast love in the morning,
    and your faithfulness by night.
For you, O LORD, have made me glad by your work;
at the works of your hands I sing for joy.
    How great are your works, O LORD!
    Your thoughts are very deep!
The dullard cannot know, the stupid cannot understand this:
though the wicked sprout like grass and all evildoers flourish,
they are doomed to destruction forever,
    but you, O LORD, are on high forever.
    You alone are worthy of praise!

OPENING PRAYER

O LORD our God, the rock of our salvation: you are upright and there is no unrighteousness in you! You make the righteous flourish like the palm tree and grow like the cedar. They are planted in your house, O LORD, and flourish in your courts, O God. In old age they still produce fruit; they are always fresh and green! O LORD Most High, draw near and refresh us with your Holy Spirit! Pour fresh oil over your elect, as we consider how Jesus was anointed for his burial and the Holy Lamb of God was prepared for the sacrifice by which he has saved those who receive him and believe in his name. Let our thoughts be instructed by your thoughts, let our hopes be stirred by the remembrance of your great and mighty works, and let this service of worship be our outpouring of love for you, for we seek your presence, O God, the presence of Christ Jesus and of all your elect; we have come to worship you at the appointed time and place, with the hope that you, our God, will bless us in all our undertakings, as we learn to exercise the authority of faith in the love of Jesus Christ.

CALL TO CONFESSION

Scripture says, give the adversary no occasion to revile you, for some have already turned away. Do not participate in the sins of others, but keep yourselves pure. The sins of some people are conspicuous and precede them to judgment, while the sins of others follow them there. So also good works are conspicuous, and even when they are not, they cannot remain hidden. As for those who persist in sin, they stand exposed in the sight of God, that the rest may stand in the fear of the Lord, for the enemies of the Lord shall perish and all evildoers shall be scattered. Friends, let us confess and seek purification for our sins.

PRAYER OF CONFESSION

O God our Redeemer, you have commanded that we appear before you regularly to offer you gifts in proportion to the blessings we have received and to remember all that you have done to set us free from the power of sin. Yet we confess that we have kept faith neither with you nor with those whom you have entrusted to us. The poor are always with us, yet we grow forgetful of their plight. We have received much from our elders, yet we have not shown proper respect or gratitude. We have neglected our duty to family, friends, and neighbors, and most of all, we have failed to conduct ourselves and choose our words with a proper awareness of your watchful presence. We have allowed sensual desires to alienate us from Christ. Forgive us, O Lord! Help us put an end to idleness, gossip, and harsh words, and help us to regard one another impartially as beloved members of your family, to treat one another with absolute purity, and to give honor to whom honor is due. Give us

grace to do what we can to express our love for you by showing kindness and love, humility and generosity, understanding and forgiveness to the members of your household and to all whom we meet; in Jesus' name.

DECLARATION OF FORGIVENESS

Remember that you were once a slave in Egypt, but now you have set your hope on God! For God has provided Christ Jesus as the Lamb to preserve and protect you from the angel of death. Therefore, continue in prayers and supplications, and diligently observe the statutes of the LORD. Do not live for pleasure, but always be above reproach. Help the afflicted, show hospitality to the saints, provide for your family, and in so doing you will ensure that you do not deny the faith. Let your good works be well attested and devote yourselves to them in every way. Manage your households well, so as to avoid burdening the church with responsibilities that should be met at home. Let elders, teachers, and those in authority be considered worthy of double honor. In this way, with pure speech and upright conduct, you who have been forgiven and redeemed shall proclaim the gospel of Jesus Christ in the whole world! Hear, believe, and tell the goods news! In Jesus Christ we are forgiven.

THE REAFFIRMATION OF THE BAPTISMAL COVENANT

A READING OF THE TEN COMMANDMENTS [Deuteronomy 5:1–21]

Hear, O Israel, the statutes and ordinances that I am addressing to you today; you shall learn them and observe them diligently. The LORD our God made a covenant with us at Horeb. Not with our ancestors did the LORD make this covenant, but with us, who are all of us here alive today. The LORD spoke with you face to face at the mountain, out of the fire. . . . And he said:

I am the LORD your God, who brought you out of the land of Egypt, out of the house of slavery; you shall have no other gods before me.

You shall not make for yourself an idol, whether in the form of anything that is in heaven above, or that is on the earth beneath, or that is in the water under the earth. You shall not bow down to them or worship them; for I the LORD your God am a jealous God, punishing children for the iniquity of parents, to the third and fourth generation of those who reject me, but showing steadfast love to the thousandth generation of those who love me and keep my commandments.

You shall not make wrongful use of the name of the LORD your God, for the LORD will not acquit anyone who misuses his name.

Observe the Sabbath day and keep it holy, as the LORD your God commanded you. Six days you shall labor and do all your work. But the seventh day is a Sabbath to the LORD your God; you shall not do any work—you, or your son or your daughter, or your male or female slave, or your ox or your donkey, or any of your livestock, or the resident alien in your towns, so that your male and female slave may rest as well as you. Remember that you were a slave in the land of Egypt, and the LORD your God brought you out from there with a mighty hand and an outstretched arm; therefore the LORD your God commanded you to keep the Sabbath day.

Honor your father and your mother, as the LORD your God commanded you, so that your days may be long and that it may go well with you in the land that the LORD your God is giving you.

You shall not murder.

Neither shall you commit adultery.

Neither shall you steal.

Neither shall you bear false witness against your neighbor.

Neither shall you covet your neighbor's wife.

Neither shall you desire your neighbor's house, or field, or male or female slave, or ox, or donkey, or anything that belongs to your neighbor.

PROFESSION OF FAITH

Beloved in Christ, the one baptism that we all share is the sign and seal of our cleansing from sin, our having died with Christ and our having been raised with him into eternal life and grafted into his body, the church, of which he is the head and supreme authority. Through the birth, life, death, and resurrection of Jesus Christ, the power of sin is broken and God's kingdom has entered the world. Through baptism we have been made citizens of the kingdom where Christ is King of kings and Lord of lords, who has abolished death and brought life and immortality to light through the gospel. Therefore, guard the good treasure entrusted to you, with the help of the Holy Spirit living in you. Let us reaffirm, in the presence of God, our desire to keep the baptismal covenant that God has established by his grace and by which we choose to serve Almighty God, who chose us before the foundation of the world to receive salvation, mercy, and blessing. I therefore ask you to reject sin, to profess your faith in Christ Jesus, and to confess the faith of the whole church, the faith in which we were baptized:

Trusting in the gracious mercy of God, do you turn from the ways of sin and renounce evil and its power in the world?

I do.

Do you turn to Jesus Christ, and accept him as your Savior and Lord, trusting in his grace, mercy, and love?

I do.

Will you be Christ's faithful disciple, obeying his word and showing his love? And will you devote yourself to scriptural teaching, to the church's fellowship, to the breaking of bread, and to the prayers?

I will, with God's help.

THE APOSTLES' CREED

Let us publicly profess what we believe:

> **I believe in God the Father Almighty,**
> **Maker of heaven and earth;**
> **and in Jesus Christ, his only Son our Lord,**
> **who was conceived by the Holy Ghost,**
> **born of the Virgin Mary,**
> **suffered under Pontius Pilate,**
> **was crucified, dead, and buried;**
> **he descended into hell;**
> **the third day, he rose again from the dead,**
> **he ascended into heaven,**
> **and sitteth on the right hand of God the Father Almighty;**
> **from thence he shall come to judge the quick and the dead.**
> **I believe in the Holy Ghost,**
> **the holy catholic church, the communion of saints,**
> **the forgiveness of sins,**
> **the resurrection of the body,**
> **and the life everlasting. Amen.**

PRAYER OF REDEDICATION AND THE PASSING OF THE PEACE

Proper 20
Ordinary Time 25 / September 18–24

Isaiah 1:1–20

Psalm 25:11–22

John 13:1–20

Titus 1

CALL TO WORSHIP [see Isaiah 1; Titus 1]

Hear, O heavens, and listen, O earth! For the LORD has spoken:
Wash yourselves and make yourselves clean!
> For the sake of the faith of the elect and
> for the knowledge of the truth in accordance with godliness, . . .
remove evil things from before my eyes; cease to do evil, learn to do good;
seek justice, rescue the oppressed, defend the orphan, plead for the widow.
> We shall live in the hope of eternal life that God,
> who never lies, promised before the ages began!
"What to me is the multitude of your sacrifices?" says the LORD;
"I take no delight in the blood of bulls and goats!"
> But we have been entrusted by the command of the Savior
> with the proclamation of his revealed Word!
> Let us worship and serve the Living God!

OPENING PRAYER

O God our Father, who has given all things into the hands of your Son
and our Savior, we are here at your bidding to give you thanks and praise
and honor and glory for all that you have done for us through Jesus, who
came from you and has returned to you, having loved his own, and having
left us an example to follow until his return. We thank you, O God, that

your Son, our Lord, who was and is One with you and the Holy Spirit, lowered himself, taking the form of a servant, and washed the feet of his followers. O Lord, our God, we extol you and lift up your name! Yet, we also humbly ask that you would condescend once again to come down and sojourn with us, to remain with us and strengthen us, to refresh and renew us by the sheer goodness of your presence, by the Spirit of truth and love whom we have heard and known in our Servant Lord. Inspire our listening and motivate us to do those things that we know are right, that we might discover the blessings to be found in doing them. This we ask in Jesus' name, and for your glory.

CALL TO CONFESSION

The LORD has spoken: I reared children and brought them up, but they have rebelled against me. Ah, sinful nation, people laden with iniquity, children who deal corruptly, who have forsaken the LORD, who are utterly estranged! Why do you continue to rebel? The whole head is sick, and the whole heart is faint. From the sole of the foot to the head, there is no soundness in it, but bruises and sores and bleeding wounds; they have not been drained, or bound, or softened with oil. Come now, let us argue it out, says the LORD: though your sins are like scarlet, they shall be like snow; though they are red like crimson, they shall become like wool. If you are willing and obedient, you shall eat the good of the land; but if you refuse and rebel, you shall be devoured; for the mouth of the LORD has spoken. Friends, let us confess our sins and be set free from them by the steadfast love and the mercy of our God.

PRAYER OF CONFESSION [see Psalm 25:11–22]

For your name's sake, O LORD, pardon my guilt, for it is very great. My eyes are ever toward you, O LORD; turn and be gracious to me, for I am lonely and afflicted; my heart is contrite and I renounce all that offends you. May integrity and uprightness preserve me, for I wait for you. Relieve the troubles of my heart, and bring me out of my distress. Consider the afflictions and troubles of your servant, and forgive all my sins. Consider how many forces tempt and oppose and seek to make your people stumble! O guard and deliver the lives of your elect; do not let those who bear your name be put to shame, for you are our refuge. Redeem your children, O God, out of all their troubles. Wash and

cleanse us, that we may share with you in your ministry of redemption and service. We ask this in the name of Jesus Christ, your Son, our Redeemer.

Declaration of Forgiveness

"Who are they that fear the LORD? He will teach them the way that they should choose. They will abide in prosperity, and their children shall possess the land. The friendship of the LORD is for those who fear him, and he makes his covenant known to them." Your Lord and Teacher has washed you, and thus set you an example, that you also should do for others as he has done for you. Your Savior has forgiven you, and likewise set you an example, for servants are not greater than their master, nor are messengers greater than the one who sent them. If you know these things, you are blessed if you do them. To the pure all things are pure, but to the corrupt and unbelieving nothing is pure. Their very minds and consciences are corrupted. They profess to know God, but they deny him by their actions. But as for you, be neither arrogant nor quick-tempered, neither violent nor greedy for gain; but be blameless, hospitable, a lover of goodness, prudent, upright, devout, and self-controlled. Take hold of the word that is trustworthy in accordance with the gospel, that you may not only believe it, but be able to proclaim it with sound doctrine and to refute those who contradict it. For in Jesus Christ, we are truly forgiven, and by his grace we are saved.

❈ *The Passion of Our Lord Jesus Christ* ❈

Proper 21
Ordinary Time 26 / September 25–October 1

Haggai 1:1–14 (15)

Psalm 136

John 13:21–38

Ephesians 5:21–33; 6:1–9 (10–20) 21–24

CALL TO WORSHIP [see Psalm 136]

O give thanks to the LORD, for he is good,
for his steadfast love endures forever;
> who alone does great wonders,
> who by understanding made the heavens,
who spread the earth upon the waters, who made the great lights,
the sun to rule the day, the moon and stars to rule the night,
> who brought Israel out from Egypt,
> with a strong hand and an outstretched arm,
> who divided the Red Sea,
> and made Israel pass through the midst of it.
It is he who remembers us in our low estate,
and rescues us from our foes.
> O give thanks to the God of heaven,
> for his steadfast love endures forever!

OPENING PRAYER

Our Lord Jesus Christ, you who were betrayed, denied, and abandoned by
those closest to you, for all this, you have been glorified by the Father and
the Father has been glorified in you. For all this, your love is not diminished, but rather, because you and the Father and the Spirit are Love itself,

183

you left this earth having issued a new commandment, that love should increase, that we should love one another, and further, that we should love one another just as you have loved us. Come down, divine Love! Impart yourself to us, that we may indeed be built up in love, with love, to love, and for love. For by this, by love, everyone shall know that we belong to you, who, though betrayed, denied, and abandoned, are nevertheless the glorious Lord of Love!

CALL TO CONFESSION

Thus says the LORD of hosts: Is it time for you yourselves to live in your paneled houses, while my house lies in ruins? Consider how you have fared. You have sown much and harvested little; you earn wages in order to put them into a bag with holes. Consider how you have fared! Build my house, so that I may take pleasure in it and be honored, says the LORD. You have looked for much, and it has come to little; when you brought it home, I blew it away. Why? Because my house lies in ruins, while all of you hurry off to your own houses. Therefore, the heavens above you have withheld the dew, and the earth has withheld its produce. Let the remnant of the people fear the LORD and obey his voice. Let the Holy Spirit inspire us to confess sin and devote ourselves to the work of the LORD, to work on God's house and for his household!

PRAYER OF CONFESSION

Holy God, you have called us to be subject to one another out of reverence for Christ, to be subject to one another as we are to the Lord. Yet we, your church, resist subjection even to Christ! How much less have we humbled ourselves before one another. We, the members of your body, have not shown your body the tender care it requires, nor have we nourished and loved our own bodies as is best for them. You have likened the love you would see in your church to the intimate love and loyalty of husband and wife, yet we confess that all is not right in our dearest relationships, and we are far from applying this faithful love to your church. There is disobedience, pride, provocation, and anger among us, but little discipline, obedience, or instruction in the Lord. Rather than doing your will for your pleasure and with singleness of heart, we render service with little enthusiasm. Forgive us, Lord! Make us mindful that we serve you alone, who have given Christ Jesus to

suffer and die for us; we do not labor for human approval, but knowing that whatever good we do, we will receive the same again from you, for you are the Lord over all, and with you there is no partiality. Yes, forgive and inspire us, in Jesus' name!

Declaration of Forgiveness

Let the mystery of the gospel go forth! Jesus Christ loves the church and has given himself up for her, in order to make her holy by cleansing her with the washing of water and his powerful word, so as to present the church to himself in splendor, without any imperfection—yes, so that she may be holy and without blemish. Therefore, be strong in the Lord and in the strength of his power. Put on the whole armor of God, so that you may be able to stand against the wiles of the devil. For our struggle is not against enemies of blood and flesh, but against the rulers, against the authorities, against the cosmic powers of this present darkness, against the spiritual forces of evil in the heavenly places. Therefore take up the whole armor of God, so that you may be able to withstand on that evil day, and having done everything, to stand firm. Stand, therefore, and fasten the belt of truth around your waist; put on the breastplate of righteousness. Put on your feet whatever will make you ready to proclaim the gospel of peace. With all of these, take the shield of faith, with which you will be able to quench all the flaming arrows of the evil one. Take the helmet of salvation, and the sword of the Spirit, which is the word of God. Pray in the Spirit always in every prayer and supplication. To that end keep alert and always persevere in supplication for all the saints. For I declare to you the mystery of the gospel: in Jesus Christ, we are truly forgiven and redeemed! Peace be to the whole church, and love with faith, from God the Father and the Lord Jesus Christ. Grace be with all who have an undying love for our Lord Jesus Christ.

Proper 22
Ordinary Time 27 / October 2–8
(World Communion Sunday)

2 Chronicles 7:1–22 (OR Haggai 1:15–2:9)

Psalm 41 OR 44

Matthew 26:20–35 OR Mark 14:17–31 OR Luke 22:14–38

Colossians 3:18—4:18

CALL TO WORSHIP

Give thanks to the LORD, for he is good,
for his steadfast love endures forever!
> **Let your glory come and fill this place!**
> **Let the light of your countenance shine upon us!**
For not in my bow do I trust, O LORD, nor can my sword save me.
But in you we boast continually, and we will give thanks to your name forever.
> **We have heard with our ears, our ancestors have told us,**
> **what deeds you performed in the days of old!**
For not by their own swords did they win the land,
nor did their own arm give them victory;
> **but your right hand, and the light of your countenance,**
> **for you, our God and King, command victory for your elect!**

OPENING PRAYER

O God our Father, who sent Jesus Christ, the Great Shepherd of the sheep, to fulfill the Passover through his suffering, coming among us as one who serves, giving his body and shedding his blood in order to establish a new covenant with all who are called by his name: Strengthen us, we pray, that our faith may never fail. Nourish us that we may encourage one another. Help us recognize the many talents and provisions with which you have blessed us, and teach us to dedicate and use them to the service of your kingdom. Neither let us overlook or neglect or shy away from the offering of ourselves. For truly you, our Passover Lamb, have provided all things needful, giving even of your flesh and blood for our salvation, thereby showing your grace and goodness to sinners. Thank you, O Lord, for the body and blood of Christ, by which your Spirit imparts grace to us and builds us up to be the body of Christ. Come, O Lord our God, Father, Son and Holy Spirit, come and receive our thanks and praise!

CALL TO CONFESSION

The LORD has promised: "When I shut up the heavens so that there is no rain, or command the locust to devour the land, or send pestilence among my people, if my people who are called by my name humble themselves, pray, seek my face, and turn from their wicked ways, then I will hear from heaven, and will forgive their sin and heal their land. Now my eyes will be open and my ears attentive to the prayer that is made in this place." Surely God is in this place, and he alone knows the secrets of the heart. Let us humble ourselves in confession.

PRAYER OF CONFESSION

We confess, O LORD, that we have not followed you wholeheartedly, nor have we loved one another as you have loved us. We have feared scarcity, failing to trust in your provision. We have suffered disgrace, and our sins have covered us with shame. Yet we have not forgotten you, and our hearts have not turned back. Though you have broken us and covered us with deep darkness, yet we will trust in you. Though we may be killed all day long and counted as sheep for the slaughter, yet we know that Christ Jesus, your Son, has gone this way before. He has paid the ultimate price for us, has called us to follow him and to calculate the cost. Therefore, rise up, O God of the covenant! Forgive our sins and come quickly to our aid. Redeem us for the sake of your steadfast love. For we are sunk very low and our bodies cling to the dust. Rouse yourself, O LORD! Do not cast us off forever! For though the world offers up many gods, we call upon you, knowing that you alone are the God who saves, and you will rescue us unharmed from the battles that

we wage. Therefore, we have hope in you and in the name of your Son, Jesus Christ.

DECLARATION OF FORGIVENESS

Who is left among you that saw this house in its former glory? How does it look to you now? Is it not in your sight as nothing? Yet now take courage, says the LORD; take courage, all you people of the land. Work, for I am with you, says the LORD of hosts, according to the promise that I made you when you came out of Egypt. My spirit abides among you; do not fear. For once again, in a little while, I will shake the heavens and the earth and the sea and the dry land; and I will shake all the nations, so that the treasure of all nations shall come, and I will fill this house with splendor, says the LORD of hosts. The silver is mine, and the gold is mine. The latter splendor of this house shall be greater than the former, and in this place I will give prosperity, says the LORD of hosts. Therefore, devote yourselves to prayer, keeping alert in it with thanksgiving. At the same time, pray that God will open a door for the word, that the mystery of Christ may be clearly revealed. Conduct yourselves wisely toward outsiders, making the most of the time. Let your speech always be gracious, seasoned with salt, so that you may know how you ought to answer everyone. As fellow servants in the Lord, encourage one another's hearts, always praying on behalf of those who would stand mature and fully assured in everything that God wills. For this is God's will for all who trust in his beloved Son, Jesus Christ, in whom we have redemption, the forgiveness of our sins.

THE SACRAMENT OF THE LORD'S SUPPER

THE INVITATION

Jesus said: "I have eagerly desired to eat this Passover with you before I suffer; for I tell you, I will not eat it until it is fulfilled in the kingdom of God." Then he took a cup, and after giving thanks he said, "Take this and divide it among yourselves; for I tell you that from now on I will not drink of the fruit of the vine until the kingdom of God comes" (Luke 22:15–18). And the Spirit says, "Clean out the old yeast so that you may be a new batch, as you really are unleavened. For our paschal lamb, Christ, has been sacrificed. Therefore, let us celebrate the festival, not with the old . . . yeast of malice and evil, but with the unleavened bread of sincerity and truth" (1 Cor 5:7–8). Our Good Shepherd, our High Priest, our Passover Lamb, the Lord Jesus Christ invites all who trust in him to partake of this feast that he has prepared.

THE GREAT THANKSGIVING

Thank you, Holy Lord, for your plenteous provision to your whole creation. For you open your hand, satisfying the desire of every living thing. You visit the earth and water it, you greatly enrich it; the river of God is full of water; you provide the people with grain, for so you have prepared it. You water its furrows abundantly, settling its ridges, softening it with showers, and blessing its growth. You crown the year with your bounty; even your wagon tracks overflow with richness. The pastures of the wilderness overflow, the hills gird themselves with joy, the meadows clothe themselves with flocks, the valleys deck themselves with grain, they shout and sing together for joy. All creatures look to you, to give them their food in due season; when you give to them, they gather it up; when you open your hand, they are filled with good things. When you hide your face, they are dismayed; when you take away their breath, they die and return to their dust. When you send forth your spirit, they are created; and you renew the face of the ground.

Thank you, O God our Father, for though we have often chosen sin over freedom, you have delivered us from slavery with a strong arm and an outstretched hand; though we are stubborn and slow to realize the length and breadth and height and depth of your redeeming love for us and how long you have been planning our redemption, yet you have decreed that we should keep the Passover throughout our generations as a perpetual ordinance, fulfilled and transformed, as it is, into a new covenant, a sacrament by which to enjoy and partake of your real, holy presence.

Thank you, O Christ the Son, for the eager longing with which you come to meet us in this feast, for sharing with us your divine substance, the living bread, the eternal life that is borne to us in your body and your blood. What longing you awaken in us to see you as you truly are, to know you fully even as we are fully known!

Thank you, Holy Spirit, for being the seal and the promise of our redemption, given in baptism, and renewed each time we share the bread and the cup. Thank you for endowing us with gifts, gifts with which to build up your church in truth and in love.

Therefore, Holy, Holy, Holy God, pour out your Spirit upon this bread and this wine, that the bread we break and the cup we bless may be for us the communion of the Supper of our Lord Jesus Christ, a memorial of what he has done for us and a foretaste of the heavenly wedding banquet that we will share with him, when we drink the wine anew in the kingdom of heaven.

O Lord, as we are truly one with you in body and in spirit, please tenderly care for those members of your body whom we mention to you by name, or in the quiet of our own hearts:

Bless, we pray, . . .

These things we ask in the name of our Lord Jesus Christ, who taught us when praying to say . . .

THE LORD'S PRAYER

THE WORDS OF INSTITUTION

THE SHARING

"The bread that we break, is it not a sharing in the body of Christ? Because there is one bread, we who are many are one body, for we all partake of the one bread."

"The cup of blessing that we bless, is it not a sharing in the blood of Christ?" (1 Cor 10:16–17)

THE CLOSING PRAYER

Proper 23
Ordinary Time 28 / October 9–15

Haggai 2:10–19

Psalm 3 AND 134

Matthew 26:36–56 OR Mark 14:32–52 OR Luke 22:39–53 OR John 18:1–12

Romans 7:1–12

CALL TO WORSHIP

Come, bless the LORD, all you servants of the LORD,
who stand in the house of the LORD!
> **You, O LORD, are a shield around me,**
> **my glory, and the one who lifts up my head!**
Lift up your hands to the holy place,
and bless the LORD.
> **I cry aloud to the LORD, and he answers me from his holy hill.**
> **I lie down and sleep; I wake again, for the LORD sustains me.**
Be not afraid if ten thousands of people set themselves against you all around.
May the LORD, maker of heaven and earth, bless you from Zion!
> **Rise up, O LORD! Deliver me, O my God!**
> **For deliverance belongs to the LORD!**
> **May your blessing be on your people!**

OPENING PRAYER

Almighty Father, who inspired the Scriptures by the Holy Spirit and fulfilled them in your obedient Son, Jesus Christ, how can we thank you enough for what you have done to bring humankind under your heavenly reign? For what we have not been able to do for ourselves, Christ has done for us, through his passion and his struggle in the garden, subjecting his human nature to his divine will and yours, longing to have the cup pass from him, knowing that more than twelve legions of angels stood ready to rescue him, yet foregoing these things and submitting himself to the sentence that you had pronounced on sin. He gave himself up to those who would put him to death, and thus showed how ultimately weak and empty are the powers of darkness. Almighty Father, how can we thank you enough for what you have done to bring us back into fellowship with you through the suffering of your Son? Let us not fall asleep, as though unaware of your presence among us or your goodwill toward us! For though our spirits are willing, we admit our flesh is weak; though our eyes grow heavy with depressing worldly concerns, you have summoned us to pray that we might not fall into temptation or come to the time of trial. Therefore, come among us with your awakening Spirit and your strengthening power. Allow us, we pray, for your name's sake, to praise you for all that you have done for our sake. This we ask of you, our loving Father, in the mighty name of Jesus.

Call to Confession

Hear and understand the purpose of the law. For the law is binding on a person only during that person's lifetime. When one dies, one is free from the law. While we were living in the flesh, our sinful passions, aroused by the law, were at work in our members to bear fruit for death. What then should we say? That the law is sin? By no means! Yet, if it had not been for the law, we would not know sin. We would not have known what it is to covet if the law had not said, "You shall not covet." But sin, seizing an opportunity in the commandment, produces all kinds of covetousness. Apart from the law sin lies dead. Once we were alive apart from the law, but when the commandment came, sin revived and, seizing an opportunity in the commandment, has deceived and killed. Thus, we have died, for the very commandment that promised life proves to be death to sinners. In the same way, you have died to the law through the body of Christ, so that you may belong to another, to him who has been raised from the dead in order that you may bear fruit for God. Therefore, in the hope of new life, let us confess our sins.

PRAYER OF CONFESSION [Adapted from the Jewish Prayer *Avinu Malkenu*]

Our Father, our King, we have sinned before you.

Our Father, our King, we have no king beside you and your Son,
Jesus Christ, who is seated at the right hand of power.

Our Father, our King, have mercy upon us for your name's sake.

Our Father, our King, nullify all evil decrees against us.

Our Father, our King, frustrate the plans of those who hate us,
whether they be spirit, or merely flesh and blood,
for what can flesh and blood do to those who love and fear you,
and what spirit can defy your authority
when we take every thought captive for obedience to Christ?

Forgive us, O LORD; forgive and bless us.

For we offer you this prayer in Jesus' name.

DECLARATION OF FORGIVENESS [see Haggai 2:10–19]

Truly, the law is holy, and the commandment is holy and just and good.
But now we are discharged from the law, dead to that which held us captive, so that we are slaves not under the old written code but in the new life of the Spirit! Ask the priests for a ruling: When one carries what is holy in the fold of one's garment, and with the fold touches something, it does not become holy. And if one touches anything unholy, one becomes unclean. Yet this is not the way it is with Christ, who touches the unclean and makes them clean, who was arrested as though he was a bandit and was crucified as though he was a thief, in order that his redemption should be unambiguously on behalf of sinners! Therefore, consider what will come to pass from this day on. Before a stone was placed upon a stone in the LORD's temple, how did you fare? When one came to a heap of twenty measures, there were but ten; when one came to the well to draw fifty measures, there were but twenty. All the products of your toil were stricken with blight and mildew and hail; yet you did not return to me, says the LORD. Consider from this day on, since the day that the foundation of the LORD's temple was laid, consider: Is there any seed left in the barn? Do the vine, the fig tree, the pomegranate, and the olive tree still yield nothing? From this day forth, I will bless you, says the LORD.

Proper 24
Ordinary Time 29 / October 16–22

Haggai 2:20–23 OR Daniel 7: (1–3) 4–14 (15–18) 19–28

Psalm 38 OR 55

Matthew 26:57–27:1–2 OR Mark 14:53–15:1 OR Luke 22:54–23:1 OR John 18:13–28

Romans 9:6–33

CALL TO WORSHIP

The word of the LORD has come, saying:
"I am about to shake the heavens and the earth."
As I watched, the Ancient of Days took his throne;
his clothing was white as snow,
and fire flowed out from his presence.
"I am about to overthrow the throne of kingdoms,
to destroy the strength of the nations."
The court sat in judgment, and the books were opened;
and I saw one like a Son of Man coming with the clouds of heaven.
"On that day, I will take you, my servant, and make you like a signet ring;
for I have chosen you, says the LORD of hosts."
And he came to the Ancient of Days and was presented before him.
To him was given glory and everlasting dominion, that all should
serve him, and a kingdom that shall never pass away.

OPENING PRAYER

O Blessed God, what a wondrous thing it is that you have sent your Son
to be the stone over which people stumble, to cause us to reflect, to think
and consider and ask who Jesus is and what he has done for us. Though

false testimonies were uttered against him; though he was wrongly charged with blasphemy; though beaten and blindfolded, spat upon and sentenced to death; though denied even by his nearest disciple, Jesus is indeed the Christ, the Son of the Living God. Now seated at the right hand of power, he shall come with the clouds of heaven, and—thanks be to God!—we shall see him as he truly is. And, according to your promise, we shall be like him! Hear our prayer, O Blessed God! Hear and draw near, that we might properly give you thanks and praise for Jesus Christ, the Chosen One, in whom we place our hope and faith!

CALL TO CONFESSION

Who are human beings to argue with God? Will what is molded say to the one who molds it, "Why have you made me like this?" Has the potter no right over the clay, to make out of the same lump one object for special use and another for ordinary use? What if God, desiring to show his wrath and to make known his power, has endured with much patience the objects of wrath that are made for destruction; and what if he has done so in order to make known the riches of his glory for the objects of mercy, which he has prepared beforehand for glory? As he says in Hosea, "Those who were not my people I will call 'my people,' and her who was not beloved I will call 'beloved.'" "And in the very place where it was said to them, 'You are not my people,' there they shall be called children of the living God." It is not as though the word of God has failed. For not all of Abraham's children are his true descendants; but "it is through Isaac that descendants shall be named for you." This means that it is not the children of the flesh who are the children of God, but the children of the promise are counted as descendants. What then are we to say? Is there injustice on God's part? By no means! For he says, "I will have mercy on whom I have mercy, and I will have compassion on whom I have compassion." So it depends not on human will or work, but on God who shows mercy, for he has mercy on whomever he chooses, and he hardens the heart of whomever he chooses. Let us therefore confess our sins and appeal for God's mercy.

PRAYER OF CONFESSION [Psalm 38]

O LORD, we confess there is no soundness in our flesh because of your indignation; there is no health in our bones because of our sin. Our

iniquities have overwhelmed us; they weigh like a burden too heavy to bear. Our wounds grow foul because of our foolishness. We are utterly bowed down and prostrate; we go around in mourning. Yet, all our longing is known to you; our sighing is not hidden from you. Our hearts throb, our strength fails, and the light of our eyes grows dim. But it is for you, O LORD, that we wait; it is you, our God, who will answer. For we confess our iniquity and we are sorry for our sin. Do not forsake us, O LORD our God; do not be far away. Forgive us, O God; make haste to help us, for you alone are strong to save. We ask in Jesus' name.

DECLARATION OF FORGIVENESS

What are we to say? Those who did not strive for righteousness have attained righteousness through faith; but those who did strive for the righteousness that is based on the law, did not succeed in fulfilling that law, because they did not strive for it on the basis of faith, but as though it were based on works. They have stumbled over the stumbling stone, as it is written, "See, I am laying in Zion a stone that will make people stumble, a rock that will make them fall, and whoever believes in him will not be put to shame." Surely, righteousness comes when we place our faith in Christ, and the Lord will not permit the righteous to be moved. Trust, therefore, in the Lord Jesus Christ, for in Jesus Christ we are forgiven.

≪ The Passion of Our Lord Jesus Christ ≫

Proper 25
Ordinary Time 30 / October 23–29

Nahum 1:1–8

Psalm 33: (1–12) 13–22

Matthew 27:3–31a OR Mark 15:2–20a OR Luke 23:2–25 OR John 18:29–19:16

Romans 10:1–4, 16–21; 11:2–28 (29–32) 33–36

CALL TO WORSHIP [Psalm 33:13–22]

The LORD looks down from heaven; he sees all humankind.
From where he sits enthroned he watches all the inhabitants of the earth—
he who fashions the hearts of them all,
and observes all their deeds.
A king is not saved by his great army;
a warrior is not delivered by his great strength.
The war horse is a vain hope for victory,
and by its great might it cannot save.
Truly the eye of the LORD is on those who fear him,
on those who hope in his steadfast love,
to deliver their soul from death, and to keep them alive in famine.
Our soul waits for the LORD; he is our help and shield.
Our heart is glad in him, because we trust in his holy name.
Let your steadfast love, O LORD, be upon us,
even as we hope in you.

OPENING PRAYER

O LORD our God, you are slow to anger but great in power. Your way is in whirlwind and storm, and the clouds are the dust of your feet. You rebuke the sea and make it dry, and you dry up all the rivers. The mountains quake before you, and the hills melt; the earth heaves before you, the world and all who live in it. Who can stand before your indignation? Who can endure the heat of your anger? For your wrath is poured out like fire, and you shatter the rocks into pieces. Yet you, O LORD, are good, a stronghold in the day of trouble! You protect those who take refuge in you, even in a rushing flood. Come, then, to this sanctuary, and let your Spirit flow; let the desires of your heart be made known to us, that salvation might come according to your righteousness. Let the grace of your eternal light shine upon all who are gathered here, that we may see and know and receive salvation in Christ who, himself condemned by humankind, has become the very end of the law, that there may be righteousness for all who believe.

CALL TO CONFESSION

Not all have obeyed the good news; for faith comes from what is heard, and what is heard comes through the word of Christ. But the LORD has spoken, "All day long I have held out my hands to a disobedient and contrary people." Yet God has also said, "Out of Zion will come the Deliverer; he will banish ungodliness from Jacob. . . . And this is my covenant with them, when I take away their sins." In faith and hope and penitence, let us confess our sins and our need for deliverance by the word of Christ.

PRAYER OF CONFESSION

O LORD our God, we confess to you that we have a sluggish spirit, eyes that see little and ears that often refuse to hear. We stand in pride when we should stand in awe. We, though wild olive shoots, forget that we have been adopted, transplanted, and ingrafted; we are supported by the root, included in the tree of life, your family of faith, only by virtue of your grace and kindness. Forgive us, O LORD, for every boastful moment, every harsh or careless word; most of all, forgive us for past unbelief. Let us not be pruned or broken off, but help us stand up and glorify you in faith. For if you have not spared some of the natural branches, who are we to presume that we should be spared? Continue, O LORD, in your kindness toward us. Have mercy, O God; graciously preserve and prosper us, even as we ask your mercies for all those who know you and

call upon your name. This we ask for the sake of your Son, Jesus Christ our Lord.

Declaration of Forgiveness

God has not rejected his people whom he foreknew. Remember how Elijah pleaded with God: "Lord, they have killed your prophets, they have demolished your altars; I alone am left, and they are seeking my life." And remember God's reply: "I have kept for myself seven thousand who have not bowed the knee to Baal." So too at the present time there is a remnant, chosen by grace. But if it is by grace, it is no longer on the basis of works, otherwise grace would no longer be grace. Some have failed to obtain what they were seeking. The elect obtained it, but others were hardened. Have all those who have been hardened stumbled so as to fall? By no means! But through their stumbling salvation has come to more and more, so as to make God's people jealous. Now if their stumbling means riches for the world, how much more will Israel's full inclusion mean! For if their rejection is the reconciliation of the world, what will their acceptance be but life from the dead! If the part of the dough offered as first fruits is holy, then the whole batch is holy; and if the root is holy, then the branches also are holy. Do not claim to be wiser than you are, but understand this mystery: a hardening has come upon some, until the full number of the nations has come in. O the depth of the riches and wisdom and knowledge of God! How unsearchable are his judgments and how inscrutable his ways! "For who has known the mind of the Lord? Or who has been his counselor?" "Or who has given a gift to him, to receive a gift in return?" For from him and through him and to him are all things. To God be the glory forever. Amen.

≪ The Passion of Our Lord Jesus Christ ≫

Proper 26
Ordinary Time 31 / October 30–November 5

Nahum 1:9–15 OR Ezekiel 20:32–49

Psalm 31: (105) 6–14 (15–16) 17–24 OR 40: (1–11) 12–17

Luke 23:26–32

Romans 15:1–3, 14–33

CALL TO WORSHIP

Love the LORD, all you his saints.
> The LORD preserves the faithful,
> but abundantly repays the one who acts haughtily.
Let the lying lips be stilled that speak insolently
against the righteous with pride and contempt.
> O how abundant is your goodness, O LORD,
> that you have laid up for those who fear you,
> and accomplished for those who take refuge in you,
> in the sight of everyone!
Those who have never been told of him shall see,
and those who have never heard of him shall understand.
> For on my holy mountain, says the LORD God,
> there I will accept them, and you shall know that I am the LORD.

OPENING PRAYER

O God our Father, who sent Jesus Christ into the world, not in order to
please himself, but to graciously bear the insults that you and your saints
have endured, to put up with the failings of the weak, to bless the barren,
and to reveal your good purpose of building up those whom the enemy
seeks to tear down: Come and refresh your weary people, refresh us with

rest in your company, refresh us with the joy and the love of the Spirit. Rescue us from unbelief and inspire us to earnest prayer, that our service to you may be acceptable in your sight and give none of your saints cause for stumbling. For by your grace we have come to share in the spiritual blessings, and we would glorify your name by uniting with your holy ones in the love of Christ and in the fullness of his blessing. Come, Lord Jesus, and refresh us in the power of your Spirit, to the glory of God the Father.

CALL TO CONFESSION

Why do people plot against the LORD? He will make an end; no adversary will rise up twice. What is in your mind shall never happen—the thought, "Let us be like the nations, like the tribes of the countries, and worship wood and stone." "As I live," says the Lord GOD, "surely with a mighty hand and an outstretched arm, and with wrath poured out, I will be king over you. I will bring you out from the peoples and gather you out of the countries where you are scattered, with a mighty hand and an outstretched arm, and with wrath poured out; and I will bring you into the wilderness of the peoples, and there I will enter into judgment with you face to face. As I entered into judgment with your ancestors in the wilderness of Egypt, so I will enter into judgment with you, says the Lord GOD. I will make you pass under the staff, and will bring you within the bond of the covenant. I will purge out the rebels among you, and those who transgress against me; I will bring them out of the land where they reside as aliens, but they shall not enter the land of Israel. Then you shall know that I am the LORD. As for you, thus says the Lord GOD: Go serve your idols, every one of you now and hereafter, if you will not listen to me; but my holy name you shall no more profane with your gifts and your idols." Let us confess our sins.

PRAYER OF CONFESSION [see Psalms 31:6–14, 17–24; 40:12–17]

O LORD, deal with me for your name's sake, and not according to what my sins deserve. For evils without number have encompassed me; my iniquities have overtaken me, until I cannot see; they are more than the hairs of my head, and my heart fails me. Be gracious to me, O LORD, for I am in distress; for my life is spent with sorrow, and my years with sighing. Be pleased, O LORD, to deliver me; O LORD, make haste to help me. Let those be put to shame and confusion who seek to snatch away

my life; let those be turned back and brought to dishonor who desire
my hurt. Let those be appalled because of their shame who say to me,
"Aha, Aha!" But may all who seek you rejoice and be glad in you; may
those who love your salvation say continually, "Great is the LORD!" As
for me, I am poor and needy, but the LORD takes thought for me. You
are my help and my deliverer; do not delay, O my God. I will trust you,
O LORD, and exult and rejoice in your steadfast love, because you have
seen my affliction; you have taken heed of my adversities, and you have
set my feet in a broad place. I trust in you, O LORD; I say, "You are my
God." Blessed be the LORD, for he has wondrously shown his steadfast
love to me when I was beset as a city under siege. I said in my alarm,
"I am driven far from your sight." But you heard my supplications as I
cried to you for help.

DECLARATION OF FORGIVENESS

Be strong, and let your heart take courage, all you who wait for the LORD.
For thus says the LORD, "Though I have afflicted you, I will afflict you no
more. I will break off the yoke from you and snap the bonds that bind
you. Look! On the mountains the feet of one who brings good tidings,
who proclaims peace! Celebrate your festivals, fulfill your vows, for never
again shall the wicked invade you; they are utterly cut off." Now, therefore,
be filled with goodness, and the knowledge of the LORD, able to instruct
one another, and remind one another of the grace that God has given you.
Let your service to the gospel of God be acceptable, sanctified by the Holy
Spirit. Let no one boast of anything except what Christ has accomplished
through you to bring the nations into obedience to the gospel by word
and deed, by the power of signs and wonders, by the power of the Spirit of
God, as you proclaim the good news of Christ abroad. For you have one
foundation, Jesus Christ the Lord, in whose name I declare to you we are
forgiven. The God of peace be with all of you.

All Saints' Day
November 1 (or *First Sunday in November*)

Haggai 1:1–14 (15) OR 2 Chronicles 19:4—20:30

Psalm 107: (1–3) 10–16, 23–32 (33–37) 38–42 (43)

Matthew 27: (45–49) 50–56

3 John

CALL TO WORSHIP [see Psalm 107:1–3, 40–43]

O give thanks to the LORD, for he is good;
    for his steadfast love endures forever.
Let the redeemed of the LORD say so,
    those he redeemed from trouble
    and gathered in from the lands,
from the east and from the west,
    from the north and from the south . . .
He pours contempt on princes
    and makes them wander in trackless wastes;
but he raises up the needy out of distress,
    and makes their families like flocks.
The upright see it and are glad;
    and all wickedness stops its mouth.
Let those who are wise give heed to these things,
    and consider the steadfast love of the LORD.

OR [see 2 Chronicles 20]

Listen to me, you chosen of God!
Believe in the LORD and you will be established;

believe his prophets; sing to the LORD and praise him in holy splendor:

"Give thanks to the LORD,
for his steadfast love endures forever."

For thus says the LORD to you:
"Do not fear or be dismayed at your enemies,
for the battle is not yours; it belongs to God.
It is not for you to fight, but only to stand still
and see the victory of the LORD on your behalf."

"We will not fear or be dismayed,
for the LORD our God is with us."

OPENING PRAYER

O LORD our God, surely your Spirit rejoices when your children walk and
love one another in the truth. Draw near to us, we pray, speak to your
people and support us, that we may be faithful to the truth, that it may go
well with us in body, soul, and spirit, and that we, your church, might be
healthy coworkers with the truth, supporting those saints and servants of
the gospel who testify and journey for the sake of Christ, blessing them in
a manner worthy of your most holy name.

CALL TO CONFESSION

Why do people plot against the LORD? He will make an end; no adversary
will rise up twice. What is in your mind shall never happen. You will
never be like the nations, worshiping wood and stone. "As I live," says the
Lord GOD, "surely with a mighty hand and an outstretched arm, and with
wrath poured out, I will be king over you. I will bring you out from the
peoples and gather you out of the nations where you are scattered, with
a mighty hand and an outstretched arm, and with wrath poured out; and
I will bring you into the wilderness, and there I will enter into judgment
with you face to face. As I entered into judgment with your ancestors in
the wilderness of Egypt, so I will enter into judgment with you, says the
Lord GOD. I will make you pass under the staff, and will bring you within
the bond of the covenant. I will purge out the rebels among you, and those
who transgress against me; I will bring them out of the land where they
reside as aliens, but they shall not enter the land of Israel. Then you shall
know that I am the LORD. As for you, thus says the Lord GOD: Go serve
your idols, every one of you now and hereafter, if you will not listen to

me; but my holy name you shall no more profane with your gifts and your idols." Let us heed the LORD and return to him, let us honor his name by confessing our sins.

PRAYER OF CONFESSION

Holy and eternal God, we confess that we have not always listened to you or shown you the obedience that is consistent with faith. We claim to acknowledge your authority, but our actions and our priorities testify against us. We have spurned your counsel, bowed to idols, and buckled under temptations. We have been quick to put ourselves first, and slow to welcome and support our brothers and sisters who take the good news of your grace and proclaim it abroad. We have allowed rumor and gossip to spread within the body of your church, and failed to be mindful of the account we must render to you on the last day. Forgive us, O LORD, for these and all our sins against you and against those whom you love. Rescue us, we pray, from prisons of our own making; lead us from our distress into your blessed peace, from our disquiet into your eternal rest, in Jesus' name.

DECLARATION OF FORGIVENESS

Let us thank the LORD for his steadfast love and for his wonderful works to humankind! For even at the resurrection of our Lord Jesus Christ, the tombs of many saints were opened, their bodies were raised, and they appeared to many. The resurrection of the dead is true, and the communion of the saints is real. Therefore, let no one any longer imitate what is evil, for whoever does evil has not seen God. But imitate what is good, for, as the truth itself will testify, whoever does what is good is from God. Therefore, in peace and joy, let us extol our risen Lord in the great congregation of his people, and praise him in the assembly of all his saints.

Proper 27
Ordinary Time 32 / November 6–12

Nahum 2:1–13 OR Jeremiah 42:1–7; 43:1–7

Psalm 71:15–24

**Matthew 27:31b–56 OR Mark 15:20b–41 OR Luke 23:33–49
OR John 19:17–30**

Romans 14:13–23

CALL TO WORSHIP [Psalm 17:15–24]

I will come praising the mighty deeds of the LORD,
I will praise your righteousness, yours alone.
> **O God, from my youth you have taught me,**
> **and I still proclaim your wondrous deeds.**
So even to old age and gray hairs, O God, do not forsake me,
until I proclaim your might to all the generations to come.
> **Your power and your righteousness reach the high heavens.**
You who have done great things, O God, who is like you?
My mouth will tell of your righteous acts, of your deeds of salvation
all day long, though their number is past my knowledge.
> **My lips will shout for joy when I sing praises to you;**
> **my soul also, which you have rescued.**

OPENING PRAYER

O God our Father, whose only Son died upon the cross, beneath an in-
scription declaring him "King of the Jews," you are not only restoring the
majesty of Israel despite the ravages your people have endured, but also,
by the power of your Spirit, you have raised Jesus from the dead. He who
suffered many troubles and endured many trials, who asked forgiveness

for his executioners, who spoke of paradise on the other side of death, who entrusted his spirit into your loving hands—he has been revived and summoned from the depths of the earth. You have increased his honor who, though he was innocent, did not act to save himself; you have seated him at your right hand, and soon you will send him again to gather to himself those who belong to your eternal reign. Therefore receive, O God, our praise for your faithfulness, with songs of joy and thanksgiving! Inspire, O Holy One, our thoughts of you, that we may talk all day long of your righteous help! For where would we be or what could we do without you, our holy God, Father, Son, and Holy Spirit? But surely, you who have died, forsaken on the cross, will not forsake your people. For you are alive again eternally, and we belong to you, through the redeeming work of Jesus Christ our Lord and King.

CALL TO CONFESSION

Let us no longer pass judgment on one another, but resolve instead never to put a stumbling block or hindrance in the way of another. For nothing is unclean in itself; but it is unclean for anyone who thinks it unclean. If your conduct is injurious to another, you are no longer walking in love. Do not let your good be spoken of as evil, and do not let your actions cause the ruin of one for whom Christ died. Everything is indeed clean, but it is wrong to make others stumble or fall. Let everything, even your confession, be motivated by faith. Those who nourish doubts are condemned already, because they do not act from faith; for whatever does not proceed from faith is sin. Therefore, in penitence and faith, let us confess our sins.

PRAYER OF CONFESSION

O LORD, holy and merciful, we confess we have often misplaced our faith and sought to establish our own righteousness. We have been afraid to submit to your claim upon our lives, and thus we find ourselves as but a remnant of a once numerous people. We have been guided by self-concern, have judged one another and made one another stumble, whereas you would have us judge ourselves, confess our own sins, and build one another up in the knowledge of your saving love. Truly, O God, we stand in need of forgiveness, renewal, reform, and grace. Therefore, be gracious to us, O God, and help us to receive grace,

we pray, that we may be better able and quick to show grace toward one another in the knowledge that Jesus has given himself up to death, and now is risen and reigns on high, not only for our sake, but for the sake of our neighbors and fellow believers. Forgive us, LORD, and help us live as forgiven and forgiving people, to the honor and glory of your Son, Jesus Christ, in whose name we pray.

DECLARATION OF FORGIVENESS

Truly the kingdom of God is not food and drink but righteousness and peace and joy in the Holy Spirit. The one who thus serves Christ is acceptable to God and has human approval. Let us then pursue what makes for peace and for mutual upbuilding. The faith that you have, have as your own conviction before God. Blessed are those who have no reason to condemn themselves because of what they approve. And blessed are those who live by faith, for Christ is our faith, and in faith you are truly one with the sinless one, Jesus Christ, in whom we are forgiven and free from sin.

⤳ *The Passion of Our Lord Jesus Christ* ⤳

Proper 28
Ordinary Time 33 / November 13–19

Nahum 3:1–19 OR Zechariah 12:1–13:1

Psalm 77: (1–2) 3–10 (11–20)

Matthew 27:57–66 OR Mark 15:42–47 OR Luke 23:50–56 OR John 19:31–42

>[COMPREHENSIVE OPTION: John 19:31–37; Luke 23:50–52;
>Mark 15:44–45; John 19:39–42; Luke 23:55–56]

Romans 16:1–25 (26–27)

CALL TO WORSHIP [Zechariah 12:10—13:1]

The LORD has spoken, saying: I will pour out a spirit of compassion
and supplication on the house of David and the inhabitants of Jerusalem.
>**When they look on the one whom they have pierced,**
>**they shall mourn for him, as one mourns for an only child,**
>**and weep bitterly over him, as one weeps over a firstborn.**
On that day the mourning in Jerusalem will be as great
as the mourning in the plain of Megiddo.
>**The land shall mourn, each family by itself;**
the family of the house of David by itself,
the family of Levi by itself,
>**and all the families that are left, each by itself.**
On that day a fountain shall be opened for the house of David
and the inhabitants of Jerusalem,
>**to cleanse them from sin and impurity.**

OPENING PRAYER

Lord Jesus Christ, even in death, you, the Living Word, have spoken and offered the testimony of God, the testimony of the Spirit and the water and the blood, that the word of the LORD might not return empty. Even in death you fulfilled the prophets, preached to the spirits that were in prison, and kept the Sabbath wholly, manifesting the grace of God in the face of the abuse and disgrace that continued to be heaped upon you, even in death. Now, O Lord, now that you live again, how much more do we hope to hear from you—you, the Lord of eternal life—and how much more do we hope to be refreshed in your Holy Spirit, to see you in your glory! Meet with us, we pray, in this time and place, and speak from eternity, testify once more, that we may hear and be strengthened in faith and hope and the love of your dear name.

CALL TO CONFESSION [see Zechariah 12:1–9]

Thus says the LORD, who stretched out the heavens and founded the earth and formed the human spirit within: See, I am about to make Jerusalem a cup of reeling for all the surrounding peoples; it will be against Judah also in the siege against Jerusalem. On that day I will make Jerusalem a heavy stone for all the peoples; all who lift it shall grievously hurt themselves. And all the nations of the earth shall come together against it. On that day, I will strike every horse with panic, and its rider with madness. But on the house of Judah I will keep a watchful eye. Then they shall say to themselves, "Those in Jerusalem have strength through the LORD of hosts, their God." On that day the LORD will shield those in Jerusalem so that the feeblest among them shall be like David, and the house of David shall be like the angel of the LORD. In penitence and faith, let us confess our sins and ask the LORD to forgive, defend, and preserve us, as he will do for Jerusalem, on that day.

PRAYER OF CONFESSION

O LORD, do not spurn us forever; do not forget to be gracious. Let not your steadfast love cease or your promises go unfulfilled. For we are troubled by the state of the world, and dismayed that the world's troubles reflect the troubled state of the church and, indeed, our own souls. Forgive us, LORD, for seeking peace and respite, reconciliation and salvation, in places where they are not to be found. Forgive us for our

rebellious ways, which required the death of your Son. Forgive us for the ways in which we continue to rebel. Teach us, O LORD, how to order our lives through humble submission to your ways—holy and righteous, yet gracious and loving—which are the sure sign of your kingdom. And may your kingdom soon come to earth and be manifestly established under the lordship of Jesus Christ our Savior, who lives and reigns with you and the Holy Spirit, one God, both now and forever.

DECLARATION OF FORGIVENESS

Cause no dissension and give no one cause for stumbling, for such conduct is contrary to the teaching that you have learned, and those who do these things do not serve our Lord Christ. Rather, they serve their own appetites, and by smooth talk and flattery they deceive the hearts of the simpleminded. Instead, be wise in what is good and guileless in what is evil. Let your obedience be known to all. For the grace of our Lord Jesus Christ is with you, by whose death on the cross a fountain has been opened to cleanse you from sin and impurity. The God of peace will shortly crush Satan under your feet. Now to God who is able to strengthen you according to the gospel and the proclamation of Jesus Christ, according to the revelation of the mystery that was kept secret for long ages but is now disclosed, and through the prophetic writings is made known to all the nations, according to the command of the eternal God, to bring about the obedience of faith—to the only wise God, through Jesus Christ, be the glory forever! Amen.

Proper 29

Ordinary Time 34 / November 20–26

(*Christ the King* or *Reign of Christ*)

Obadiah 1–21

Psalm 87 AND 117

John 12:17–19, 37–50

1 Corinthians 15:27–50 (51–57)

CALL TO WORSHIP

On the holy mount stands the city he founded;
the LORD loves the gates of Zion more than all the dwellings of Jacob.
Glorious things are spoken of you, O city of God.
> Of Zion it shall be said, "This one and that one were born in it";
> for the Most High himself will establish it.
The LORD records, as he registers the peoples,
"This one was born there."
> Singers and dancers alike say, "All my springs are in you."
Praise the LORD, all you nations! Extol him, all you peoples!
For great is his steadfast love toward us,
> and the faithfulness of the LORD endures forever.
> Praise the LORD!

OPENING PRAYER

Sovereign God, King of the Universe, you have put all things in subjection under the feet of your Son, Jesus Christ, whom you have raised imperishable from the dead! His physical body, like a seed, was sown in weakness and dishonor, yet now he is raised with a spiritual body, in power and

212

glory. Though the first man, Adam, a man of dust, became a living being, Christ Jesus, the last Adam, the man of heaven, has become a life-giving spirit! And just as we have borne the image of the man of dust, so we will also bear the image of the man of heaven. For by your design and intention, O God, this perishable body must put on imperishability, and this mortal body must put on immortality, and then the saying that is written will be fulfilled: "Death has been swallowed up in victory." Thanks be to you, eternal God, for giving us the victory through Christ our King, who, in subjection to you, will fully and finally give the kingdom into your hands, and you, our God—the Father, the Son, and the Holy Spirit—shall at last be all in all!

CALL TO CONFESSION

Though you say in your heart, "Who will bring me down to the ground?" and though you soar aloft like the eagle, and though your nest is set among the stars, from there I will bring you down, for your proud heart has deceived you, says the LORD. For the day of the LORD is near. As you have done, it shall be done to you. Do not be deceived: "Bad company ruins good morals." Some people have no knowledge of God. But you are to come to a sober and right mind, and sin no more; for the sting of death is sin, and the power of sin is the law. Therefore, let us confess our sins.

PRAYER OF CONFESSION

Truly, yours is the kingdom, O LORD, and Christ Jesus is our Savior and King! Yet we confess we have loved human glory more than the glory that comes from you. Though we profess to believe in the resurrection to eternal life, we live like those who do not believe, saying, "Let us eat and drink, for tomorrow we die." We have served and exalted ourselves by neglecting and looking down on others, at times even taking satisfaction at their misfortunes. Forgive us, LORD, for the wrongs we have done to you, and to our brothers, sisters, and neighbors. Forgive us for failing to love our enemies and to pray for those who treat us with hostility. Forgive us for failing to live worthily: as subjects of your heavenly kingdom, as children and heirs of Christ our King. Let not our sinful deeds return upon our own heads. But apply the full payment of Christ's sacrifice to our sins. Give us courage, O LORD, to die every day to the temptations of the world! Help us release our grip on merely

human hopes, that we might gain what you divinely promise, intend, and command: eternal life! This we ask in Jesus' name.

DECLARATION OF FORGIVENESS

Flesh and blood cannot inherit the kingdom of God, nor does the perishable inherit the imperishable. Listen, here is a mystery! We will not all die, but we will all be changed, in a moment, in the twinkling of an eye, at the last trumpet. For the trumpet will sound, and the dead will be raised imperishable, and we will be changed. So it is with the resurrection of the dead. For Jesus said: "I have come as light into the world, so that everyone who believes in me should not remain in the darkness. I do not judge anyone who hears my words and does not keep them, for I came not to judge the world, but to save the world. The one who rejects me and does not receive my word has a judge; on the last day the word that I have spoken will serve as judge. I have not spoken on my own, but the Father who sent me has given me a commandment about what to say and what to speak. And I know that his commandment is eternal life." Friends, give thanks to God and believe in the Lord Jesus Christ, for in him we have eternal life, and in Christ is hidden our hope of glory!

Index of Scripture Readings